The 101 Greatest Bible Verses

Ancient Lessons For Success in Business, Life, Love, and More

W.J. Vincent II

SECOND EDITION

http://www.thinkmorebemore.com
http://www.101verses.com

ISBN-10: 0615912648
ISBN-13: 978-0615912646
(Think More, Be More Inc.)

DEDICATION

To my loving wife, Natalia
Gone far too soon at the age of 34;
You spent your whole life opening doors.
You lived life the way nature intended,
Instead of dying, you truly ascended.

Our Guardian Angel above you are,
Watching over us all from afar.
Thank you for loving me the way only you could,
I dedicate this book to you for helping me to be
Better than I otherwise would.

CONTENTS

DISCLAIMER

In the interest of everyone who takes the time to read this book, it should be duly noted that I do not claim to be any kind of special spiritual guru. My own path has taken many unexpected twists and turns, and I am far from being an expert example of how people should live their lives. My mistakes in life are too numerous to count, and I do not attempt to claim any kind of status as an example of how to live. Please understand that the Bible has been a great reference for me, but I am far, far from perfect. The words from the Bible are what matter here; please do not judge the greatness of the advice the Bible offers by any of the many failings of my own life.

ACKNOWLEDGMENTS

To my parents, Bill and Judy, for introducing me to the Bible with a wonderful picture Holy Bible when I was about 3 years old. I would also like to thank some of the pastors I had in my life: Pastor Dave Holling, Pastor Wilde, Pastor Rivers, Pastor Strong, and Pastor Brockmeier, to name a few. I also need to thank my children: Maria, Andrew, Tre, and Alex, all of whom remind me every day that no matter how bad things get, miracles do exist!

FOREWORD

Okay, so an interesting thing about this book, is that I started writing it initially to save my wife's life. She was diagnosed with a brain tumor that was inoperable, incurable, and untreatable by conventional medicine. We immediately started trying lots of alternative methods and researched every spare moment to find clinics around the world that might give her a chance. According to the information we were working with, we figured she had anywhere from 3 to 7 years to try and beat it.

It was going to take a lot of money, and as luck would have it, we had invested all of our savings into trying to save the business that we owned. Without any cash...and knowing we would need literally hundreds of thousands of dollars in cash to finance these medical trips we needed to take around the world for her...in a moment of inspiration from above, I was given the idea to write this book.

Everything about this idea felt right...I was sure within my heart and soul that it would provide us with a windfall that we would be happy to share with others who found themselves in a similar plight. Alas, my beautiful wife succumbed to the dreaded disease she was battling in only 3 months. Amazingly and miraculously, one could say, she had no symptoms except for headaches right up until the day that she died. In and of itself, my wife's story deserves its own book, because she found a way to beat a horrific fate...but that is a tale for another day. The one you are about to read, which was begun in an attempt to save my wife's life, is instead—ironically—saving my own. All the powerful, wondrous, inspirational messages that I had picked up over the years from reading the Bible...these are the words and wisdom that are quite literally keeping my world from tearing apart.

Regardless of one's race, religion, or creed, there are messages that can change and even save your life found within the Bible. The verses we have selected for this book are just a sample of how powerful this great book can be. On more than one occasion, the verses contained herein have pulled me back from the ledge. So, instead of you having to search for these gems of life changing-advice...we provide them for you here with some commentary to help you to think a little bit more about what they say and mean. It is my deepest wish that this book will find a way to kindle a passion for learning, living, and loving this amazing, wonderful, tragic, and incredible journey we call Life.

CHAPTER ONE
"AN INTRODUCTION TO THE BIBLE'S GREATNESS"

"It is about the Greatness of God, not the significance of man. God made man small and the universe big to say something about himself."
~John Piper

When I was a child, my family attended church on a regular basis. In fact, my mom was usually the youth choir director. She was always organizing what we called "Song Fests" and getting everyone in the church involved in different music projects. During this time, my dad was very involved in the first church that we were members of, and participated regularly in Bible studies. My own introduction to the Bible came from mostly singing about various verses and then doing a variety of creative projects during Sunday school and Bible school. As part of my Easter Sunday present when I was about 3 years old, I received a Holy Bible that had colorful pictures in it. This Bible became the starting point for a lifelong journey through the pages of this great book.

For a while as I grew older, I was obsessed with reading the Bible cover to cover, over and over again in order to learn all that it had to offer. Many times during my formative years, I can vividly recall people saying that the Bible was the greatest book ever written. Later on during my professional life, I met many multi-millionaires and several billionaires whom proclaimed that the Bible was the greatest book on success ever written as well.

It has been my experience that there are certain statements that, when made, are seldom questioned by most people. Even as a little boy, however, I always found myself questioning. I am quite certain it was more than a little annoying for my pastors to answer these questions, and more than once I heard the ever-famous phrases, "that is just the way it is," or, "you just have to take it on faith." These were popular things to say when there was no easy answer to hard and difficult questions. In any case, as the years have gone by, my respect and admiration for the power of the Bible has only grown. Many of the verses I have chosen for this book have served me well, over and over again during difficult times.

It seemed logical to me that most people would never read the Bible cover to cover. Let's face it; the prospect of reading what in the New International Version, given to me back in 1980, was 1,341 pages is just not something that gets very high on most people's to-do list. For whatever reason, I had actually personally read the Bible cover to cover more than seven different times before I had graduated high school. Each time, I was able to pick out powerful lessons, verses, scriptures, parables, etc. that provided me with powerful guidance, inspiration, and comfort during the many challenges I have faced in life.

This book and its collection of thoughts and comments are designed to be a convenient summary for people. I like to think of it as a kind of quick-reference guide for those unable to find the time to read the Bible cover to cover to discover these valuable gems for themselves. It is my hope that the powerful verses collected here will be as helpful to you in your life as they have been in my own.

In no way, shape, or form is this book intended to be the definitive guide to the Bible, nor is the list of verses here necessarily the best 101 verses for you. If you could find the time, you would be amazed at how personal a journey through the pages of the Bible can be. It is almost like magic, as sometimes different parts will speak to you in ways that only matter to you at that particular moment in your life.

For the most part, these verses have come from the New International Version Bible given to me back in 1980, unless specially noted. The 101 verses listed and discussed in this book, are without a doubt some of the best. We hope that you are able to enjoy them as much as we have.

We will break down all of the verses into the Seven Major Areas of Life. These areas represent the categories in life in which all of us should strive for success. Those categories are: Physical, Social, Emotional, Financial, Spiritual, Family, and Mental. Obviously, with this being a book about Bible verses, we could put everything under the "spiritual" category, but in order to hopefully provide greater value as a reference to use in business and in life, we will seek to define them more specifically within these areas.

Many of these amazing Bible verses can be categorized in more than one area of life, so we will be choosing the one we think fits the best; however, readers are encouraged to decide for themselves where these words of wisdom can help the most. At the end of the day that is where the true power of the Bible comes from, its ability to be exactly what each of us needs. The arguably most popular Bible verse of all time is actually not even a Bible verse at all. Personally, I was shocked to learn that the quote "The Lord helps those who help themselves" was not even a verse in the Bible. There is a lot of evidence that it originally came from an Aesop's fable back in 6th century B.C. The actual popularity of this saying, amongst Christians and Americans, most likely stems from this being quoted by Benjamin Franklin back in 1736.

Regardless, while this quote is not a real Bible verse, it does seem to be a good way to summarize a lot of the great advice that is in the Bible. Hopefully, in the future, one or two of the 101 Greatest Bible Verses will resonate enough that one of them will one day be recognized as the most popular Bible verse. Regardless, if you take the time to read these real and powerful Bible verses, we believe you too will quickly understand why so many people believe the Bible is the greatest book ever written.

CHAPTER TWO
"PHYSICAL"

"Take care of your body. It's the only place you have to live." ~ Jim Rohn

The 18th Greatest Bible Verse – Colossians 1:11

#18 – May you be strengthened with all power according to his glorious might, for all endurance and patience with joy. (Colossians 1:11)

To be strengthened with all power has always seemed like a good thing to me. This is one of my favorite sports or competition verses. When playing football or basketball during high school, this would be one that I would reference often. As a quarterback, the patience part of this verse was important for me, and we all know how valuable endurance can be in a sporting event. The little tidbit of "joy" at the end felt like a bit of advice to enjoy and have fun with that power and endurance.

Anyone who has attended sporting events knows that all of the greatest games usually go right down to the wire. When two teams or individuals are giving the game everything they have, and refusing to give up or give in, these are the moments that offer the most enjoyment in sports. Quite often, the team or individual that ends up winning in the end is the one with the most strength, endurance, and patience. Usually, with victory, they end up with the most joy as well.

Interesting Movie Fact: It has been speculated that this verse was part of the basis for the creation of the "Force" made so popular in the Star Wars Movies. (Wikipedia)

The 2nd Greatest Bible Verse – Luke 1:37

#2 – For nothing is impossible with God. (Luke 1:37)

What an amazing verse to keep in your back pocket. Pretty much anything we face in life—any challenge—this verse takes care of us. Doesn't matter whether it is business, personal, family, social, spiritual, or otherwise....this verse tells us that nothing is impossible. Granted, the world that we now live in is full of critics and skeptics. Doubters and haters abound, and have been saying things were impossible for years. Personally, I like my chances of pulling off pretty much anything when the Bible tells me that nothing is impossible.

Anytime somebody gives you a hard time about doing something....just read this verse a couple times, and trust me, you will instantly feel better about your chances of doing anything! As a specific life example, Natalia, my wife and the mother of my children, was diagnosed with an incurable, untreatable, inoperable brain tumor. Instead of accepting what was a death sentence, she chose to confront the disease head-on. Her last months on earth were some of the most amazing days of living I have ever witnessed in my life. Every day, she learned something new, played with our children, danced, and focused on healing herself. In the end, while her body may have given out, her disease never beat her. She did the impossible and really and truly LIVED her last days.

On that last fateful day when my wife Natalia was rushed to the hospital, she believed her immune system was finally ejecting the tumor from her body. She was having strokes, but she believed that she was about to be cured. When she was in the hospital bed, the neurologist had just finished reviewing her charts and asked me how long she had been bedridden. I said that she was doing "Zumba" yesterday. He told me that was impossible; according to him, she should not have been able to even stand up. Her faith in verses like this one may not have cured her disease, but it certainly allowed her to beat that disease in every other way!

Related Movie Fact: According to IMDB.com, in the iconic movie "Cool Hand Luke", the main character Luke's prison number is 37, which is a direct reference to this Bible verse.

("Cool Hand Luke" Warner Bros. 1967)

The 4th Greatest Bible Verse – Philippians 4:13

#4 – I can do all things through Christ who strengthens me. (Philippians 4:13) [From The World English Bible]

Straight up across the board, this is one of the most powerful messages that the Bible gives us. In my own life, this was one of the first verses I ever highlighted. In fact, looking over my early notes...it was the 4th verse I ever wrote down as special.

This verse could be a sports slogan, and is one of the most quoted, studied, and referenced verses of all-time from the Bible. On more than one occasion, this simple statement was something to hold onto when times were difficult. During the early days after my wife had passed away, I repeatedly turned to this verse for inspiration.

One particularly difficult moment was when my 4-year old son was crying because if I went to heaven with Mommy, he would be all alone. Comforting my child when my own world was falling apart would have been impossible without verses like this one. I have found that when things are bad, just reading a statement as powerful as this Bible verse can change your entire mindset for the better.

To my knowledge there just isn't any way to avoid the storms that life throws at us. Dark times, low moments, challenging situations are a part of life. So just remember, if you ever catch yourself doubting your ability to do something or to get through a great adversity, this verse says we can do "ALL" things!

Related Movie Quote: From the movie "Soul Surfer", two days after the main character has lost her arm to a horrific shark bite while surfing.

Bethany: "When can I surf?"

Tom: "Soon."

Bethany: "How do you know?"

Tom: "Because you 'Can do all things ...'"

Bethany: "... through Him who gives me strength."

("Soul Surfer" Sony Pictures Entertainment 2011)

The 10th Greatest Bible Verse – James 5:15

#10 – And the prayer offered in faith will make the sick person well; the Lord will raise him up. If he has sinned he will be forgiven. (James 5:15)

Countless times in life we see evidence of this verse. Having just experienced the devastation of losing my wife suddenly and unexpectedly to a brain tumor, my perspective on this is may be a little different than most people's. See, you notice that the verse says that "the Lord will raise him up." This is a key component of the verse. Sometimes, when we are sick to the point we are most assuredly going to die unless a true miracle occurs...the miracle that we get is not the one we expect.

My lovely wife Natalia was only 34 years old when she was diagnosed with a brain tumor that was incurable, untreatable by conventional methods, and terminal. We were under the impression that she had 3 to 7 years left due to how soon we had discovered it, as her only symptom had been headaches. Unfortunately, despite all our best efforts, she lived only a little more than 3 months.

The skeptics, the atheists, the critics, all will point to this as an example that prayer doesn't work. However, my wife was most assuredly "lifted up" during her last 3 months on earth. She found an inner strength, passion, and inspiration for life that was beyond anything I had ever witnessed from her in the 13 wonderful years we were together. She went after living her life and finding a cure with a dedication that has seldom been seen. Was she made well? Again, how do you interpret this? Sometimes, we are made well in a way we understand; a sickness goes away, an illness is cured. What about living the last days of your life well? Shouldn't that count for something? During her last days...my wife grew continuously closer to God...she became so full of happiness, love, and life, it was hard to believe she could have ever done more or better even if given a 100 more years to live. The miracles that we have witnessed during this time are too many to count, and have continued long after she departed this life. So, I would say to anyone...this verse rang more true in my wife's life and even more in death than one would have thought was possible.

You see, when we pray, there is always an answer, it just isn't always the one we expect or think we need. Sometimes what we get is more than we may even be able to understand until much later. However, we must know that as with all these wonderful lessons they are very real and have much power. If we will apply them in our lives, we can enjoy many blessings and miracles that will truly amaze us. My wife may not physically be here anymore, but she is not gone, and the miracles that rained upon me, my children, and our family continue to flow, raising us up as well.

Related Movie Quote: From Natalia's favorite, "Braveheart".

William Wallace: "Every man dies, but not every man really lives." ("Braveheart" Paramount 1995)

The 15th Greatest Bible Verse – Isaiah 40:30-31

#15 – Even youths grow tired and weary, and young men stumble and fall; but those who hope in the Lord will renew their strength. They will soar on wings like eagles; they will run and not grow weary, they will walk and not be faint. (Isaiah 40:30-31)

Here is another of the Bible's great sports verses. Anyone who has regularly participated in athletics will fully appreciate the power of this verse. In fact, as a former high school quarterback, basketball player, baseball player, and track and field athlete, this little verse was what I liked to call my "4th Quarter, Sudden Death, Extra Innings, Race Off, or Overtime Special."

One game in particular stands out from my senior year of football. We were one game away from the state championship and playing in a certified blizzard. We were primarily a passing team, and with visibility at near zero, we were going to be particularly challenged to move the ball that day. There was so much snow coming down, they had to stop the game every 10 minutes to clear the lines on the field. As it turned out, we ended up down 12 to 0. Our entire team never lost hope, and somehow we came back to win the game in truly dramatic fashion, 13 to 12. On a day when many people couldn't even drive to the game we definitely soared like eagles.

Although I have never been a fan of people praying to win....I am a HUGE proponent of praying that you do your best, or that you have the strength to finish the game. This is a great verse to use for that sort of inspiration.

Interesting Movie Fact: This Bible verse was used in a scene from the movie "Chariots of Fire" which is based on a true story about Olympic athletes. ("Chariots of Fire" Warner Bros. 1981)

The 28th Greatest Bible Verse – Ecclesiastes 9:10

#28 – Whatever your hand finds to do, do it with all your might, for in the grave, where you are going, there is neither working nor planning nor knowledge nor wisdom. (Ecclesiastes 9:10)

It is certainly pretty cool to see this verse as a part of the Bible. I don't remember who it was that told me you will have plenty of time to sleep when you are dead. One of my many life coaches I am sure, trying to teach me to give whatever I was doing my all.

I remember a conversation I had with my wife Natalia while we were driving on one of our last trips together. The morning sun was peaking up over the horizon, dazzling us with its splendor. It was just the two of us, and a great song was playing on the radio. At that moment, she said, "I want to live! I really, really want to live!" This verse reminds me of how deep her desire to live was. I will spend the rest of my own life trying to capture the overwhelming desire to live life to the fullest that she had. It is with the help of verses like this one that I am reminded we must give everything we have while we are still breathing, since one day—far too soon—it will be over for us too.

Related Quote: "Never throughout history has a man who lived a life of ease left a name worth remembering."
~ Theodore Roosevelt

The 29ᵗʰ Greatest Bible Verse – Proverbs 22:29

#29 – Do you see a man skilled in his work? He will serve before kings; he will not serve before obscure men.
(Proverbs 22:29)

My dad used to always say when I was growing up, "Son, if something is worth doing, then it is worth doing right." Just one of many pearls of wisdom he shared in helping to develop a solid life foundation for each of his children. This verse from the Bible shows the value of getting good at something. Far too often in life, people are in such a hurry to just get things done, they end up doing less than quality work, and far less than their best.

The people in business and life that go the extra mile to make sure they do a great job at everything they do will never have to worry; their services will always be in demand. On the other hand, the person who does an average or poor job can easily be replaced. Also, I learned at an early age that this also applied to the world of sports. The athletes who worked the hardest at the skills of the game generally did the best and of course collected the rewards and accolades as a direct result. Meanwhile, even the most talented of athletes that didn't do the work would eventually be surpassed, and never live up to their potential.

Related Quote: "I've always believed that if you put in the work, the results will come." ~ Michael Jordan

The 30th Greatest Bible Verse – Proverbs 23:20-21

#30 – Do not join those who drink too much wine or gorge themselves on meat, for drunkards and gluttons become poor, and drowsiness clothes them in rags.
(Proverbs 23:20-21)

Simple advice to follow...don't drink too much...and don't eat too much. Of course, as always for many of us, this is easier said than done. One of the great things to me about the Bible and verses like this one is that if you find this advice at an early age, it can make so much of your life better and ultimately easier.

Many of us write off the things our parents and teachers say, figuring their advice is biased, or not worth mentioning. After all, what do they really know anyways? However, it is pretty hard to argue with a book as profoundly and widely accepted as being "great", as the Bible is. My thought process on this is that it is a whole lot easier to avoid getting trapped in the drinking scene if one is aware that a statement like this comes directly from the Bible. It is a definitive message provided to all who are willing to read it. Most people know that getting drunk and overeating don't do much good for anyone. Since this advice came from what is considered to be the word of God, hopefully it will help people to listen to it better. Or at the very least, make it easier to decide to try drinking less...and eating better.

Related Quote: "The first wealth is health."
~ Ralph Waldo Emerson

The 33rd Greatest Bible Verse – Revelation 3:16

#33 – So, because you are lukewarm—neither hot nor cold—I am about to spit you out of my mouth.
(Revelation 3:16)

I heard this verse quite a few times growing up. Most of the interpretations had to do with various descriptions of you are either for something or against it....but you cannot just sit in the middle. Essentially, this verse is teaching us to take a stand.

The Bible is saying that if you are for something, then be for it with everything that you have. Likewise, if you are against something, be against it with all that you are. On the other hand, if we are unable to choose a side—if we try to stay in the middle, avoiding a choice—then we will be spit out!

These days, far too many politicians, leaders, etc., attempt to please everybody instead of actually standing for something. We must follow this advice from the Bible...for the Bible says that it is better to be for something...or against it...than to choose nothing! This is strong advice; the type of advice that can improve every aspect of our lives, if we can find the courage to follow through.

Related Quote: "Those who stand for nothing fall for anything."
~ Alexander Hamilton

The 37th Greatest Bible Verse – Matthew 11:28

#37 – Come to me, all you who are weary and burdened, and I will give you rest. (Matthew 11:28)

There have been more than a couple times during the months after my wife passed that this verse eased my life considerably. Whenever the days were too hard, the pain too much to bear, or I was simply overwhelmed, this was a nice verse to read. Sometimes reading a verse like this really does provide one with a deep sense of release.

When it becomes too much to handle, turning a challenging situation over to God is a very special sort of way to get through. In fact, the more difficult the situation and the heavier the burden, the more powerful a verse like this becomes. Hopefully, if you are facing tough times in your own life, this verse can give you the same kind of relief and help that it provided me during the darkest times of my own life.

Related Movie Quote: From "A River Runs Through It".

Norman: "My candle burns at both ends; it will not last the night. But ah my foes, and oh my friends - it gives a lovely light." ("A River Runs Through It" TriStar Pictures 1992)

The 45th Greatest Bible Verse – 2 Thessalonians 3:13

#45 – And as for you, brothers, never tire of doing what is right. (2 Thessalonians 3:13)

There have been more than a few times over the years where people have talked about getting tired of doing the right thing. Way too often, doing the right thing goes unnoticed. It can be draining to put your energy into trying to do what is right, only to have nobody care.

If you were ever one of those people, then this Bible verse sets the record straight for you—never tire of doing what is right. It is crystal clear in its conveyance of the importance of doing what is right. Don't worry about the short-term, just keep doing what is right and over the long haul of life, it will come back to you tenfold.

This is also practical advice for people in athletics and sports. Your coach is drilling you over and over again with the fundamentals, and those fundamentals are what will save you when it matters most. So never tire of doing what is right in practice either, because come game time it will pay off!

Related Movie Quote: From the movie "Bicentennial Man"

Portia: "What's right for most people in most situations isn't right for everyone in every situation. Real morality lies in following one's own heart."

("Bicentennial Man" Buena Vista & Touchstone 1999)

The 64th Greatest Bible Verse – Deuteronomy 31:6

#64 – Be strong and courageous. (Deuteronomy 31:6)

Sometimes, life gets complicated. When it does, it can be difficult to know how to handle the situations that come up. This verse from Deuteronomy gives us a game plan that we can live by. Be strong and courageous no matter how difficult the circumstances you face may be. Again, like many of these amazing Bible verses, it is not always easy to do what is advised in them.

It is an overwhelming truth that being strong and courageous in your life is a good thing, not just for you and what you must overcome, but for everyone around you as well. Your choosing to be strong and courageous may just inspire someone else to do the same.

The best example of this I have seen in my own life was when my wife was diagnosed with a brain tumor that was incurable and untreatable. She faced what was an almost certain death with a courage and strength I had never seen. This was while she was caring for a 1-year old daughter, 4-year old son, and her 13-year old brother and 15-year old sister whom we were raising on behalf of her mother, who suffered from multiple sclerosis. She left this earth setting an example that will continue to inspire for many years to come by choosing to live the words of this verse.

Related Quote: "Courage is being scared to death…and saddling up anyway." ~ John Wayne

CHAPTER THREE
"SPIRITUAL"

"If God is all you have, you have all you need."

~ Interpretation of John 14:8

The 6th Greatest Bible Verse – Matthew 17:20-21

#6 – I tell you the truth, if you have faith as small as a mustard seed, you can say to this mountain, "Move from here to there" and it will move. Nothing will be impossible for you. (Matthew 17:20-21)

This verse was the inspiration for the cover of The 101 Greatest Bible Verses. See, in reality, a mustard seed is approximately the size of a pin head; meaning it is extremely tiny. Compared to the size of your average mountain, of course, it is infinitesimally small and insignificant. For me, the interesting thing about faith is that you simply cannot have faith and doubt at the same time. You either have faith in something, or you don't; there is no in-between.

Much as the politicians and talking heads would like to convince you differently, you either have faith or you have doubt in your life – never both at the same time. In fact, one could make a reasonable argument that faith is actually the very absence of doubt in your life. Now, if we factor in just how immovable a mountain was when this verse was written, we could pretty much make the assumption that back then moving a mountain was impossible. So what this amazing little Bible verse is telling us is that if we have faith, we can accomplish the impossible. If we have zero doubt in our lives, we can do literally anything. Powerful stuff, isn't it?

In my experience, learning this verse and making it a part of your life could be the most important step toward living an exceptional life. Once again, the Bible is telling us we can do anything. May each of us find the faith necessary to move mountains in our own lives both real and imagined.

Related Movie Quote: From the movie "The Pursuit of Happyness". (This is the main character talking to his young son)

Christopher Gardner: "Hey. Don't ever let somebody tell you... You can't do something. Not even me. All right? "

Christopher: "All right."

Christopher Gardner: "You got a dream... You gotta protect it. People can't do somethin' themselves, they wanna tell you you can't do it. If you want somethin', go get it. Period."

("The Pursuit of Happyness" Columbia Pictures 2006)

The 7th Greatest Bible Verse – Matthew 18:21-22

#7 – Then Peter came to Jesus and asked, "Lord, how many times shall I forgive my brother when he sins against me? Up to seven times? Jesus answered, "I tell you, not seven times, but seventy-seven times." (Matthew 18:21-22)

This is such an important question, and an even more important answer. We have to understand the significance with the number seven, in order to truly understand the power of this verse. Seven is considered to be the holiest number, and a veritable symbol of eternal life. So seventy-seven times is essentially eternal, or in other words, infinite. This means there is not supposed to be a limit to the number of times we are willing to forgive someone.

Most of us have a limit (and a rather small one at that) on how much we are willing to forgive. We have to be willing to forgive unlimited in order to have a successful life. This doesn't mean you should continue to allow anyone to hurt you, but it does mean that we need to find it in our hearts to be more forgiving than most of us would be on our own. There is a great deal of evidence that supports the idea that the extent to which we forgive others determines directly how many times in life we ourselves will be forgiven.

Related Movie Quote: From a the movie "Into The Wild"

Ron Franz: "When you forgive, you love, and when you love, God's light shines on you." ("Into The Wild" Paramount 2007)

The 20th Greatest Bible Verse – James 1:2-3

#20 – Consider it pure joy my brothers whenever you face trials of many kinds, because you know that the testing of faith produces perseverance. (James 1:2-3)

At one time or another, all of us face difficult times in our lives. Sometimes, those challenging situations can be overwhelming. So much of what happens to us in life is not nearly as important as how we handle it is. This verse showed me that facing tough times was unavoidable, but if I can somehow find a way to appreciate the journey through those tough times, it will be so much better.

Perseverance is one of the most important traits that anyone can develop in life. Knowing that we will face tests of our faith over and over again helps to do away with the whining and complaining trap that is so easy to fall into. It is also true that once we accept that we will face trials of many kinds, we can start looking to learn from those challenges....rather than just seeking to avoid them.

Related Famous Quote: "When the going gets tough, the tough get going." ~ Knute Rockne

The 19ᵗʰ Greatest Bible Verse – Luke 11:9

#19 – "So I say to you: Ask and it will be given to you; seek and you will find; knock and the door will be opened to you." (Luke 11:9)

When I read these words as a young boy, it seemed to me that I could have anything I wanted if I just asked for it. However, some members of the clergy, parents, and other so-called experts explained to me that that was not the case. Years later, I learned that it was actually true, with regards to prayer. If you asked in the right way, it would be given to you. If you were looking for something, truly and sincerely, you would find it, and if you really wanted to, you could open any door, figuratively or otherwise.

Most people tab this under the "too good to be true" category, and for many people it is because of their lack of faith, belief, and inability to ask properly. Think of it in the way we teach manners to kids; if they don't say please, they don't get what they are asking for. With prayer, it is somewhat like that, but, this verse is very true, and very real. If we ask in the proper way, it will indeed be given to us! However, it should be duly noted that what we get is not always what we expect.

For example, my wife prayed often to beat the cancer in her brain. She undoubtedly did, living life to the fullest right up until the moment she died. As is stated several times in this book, the day before we lost her, she was doing a full "Zumba" workout.

Clearly, she really wanted to survive the cancer and live a long life, what she was given was the most and best that was possible given the circumstances. For a variety of reasons, not the least of which is the five lives she saved with her organs, her path here on earth came to an end.

But truly as she prayed to beat the disease, she undoubtedly did, going out decidedly on her own terms right up until the end. Her final conscious thoughts were that she was actually beating it, and that she would come out of the hospital fully healed. To those of us who believe in the afterlife, this was also true, just in a different way than she or any of us had hoped for.

When we pray and ask for things in the right way, with the right attitude, we ALWAYS get what we need, even though it is not always what we thought we needed or wanted. It may take some time, possibly even years, for us to have enough perspective to actually see this in situations that are particularly challenging or personal. If we do look back with wisdom and a clearer view, we will see time and time again that miracles happened in our life, often without us even realizing it!

Related Quote: "There are only two ways to live your life. One is as though nothing is a miracle. The other is as though everything is a miracle." ~ Albert Einstein

The 24ᵗʰ Greatest Bible Verse – Romans 12:21

#24 – Do not be overcome by evil, but overcome evil with good. (Romans 12:21)

This reads like your classic "Zen" piece....or the basic subplot of a million movies made since the dawn of time. I have always loved it for its simplicity. Upon further reflection, sometimes the simplest of messages can be the most powerful. How often do we see the opposite play out? People get angry, seek revenge, one thing leads to another and the next thing you know, there is an all-out war and millions of innocent people are caught up in something that could have been avoided entirely.

These are words with which we can build a life. Choosing to follow this advice can fundamentally change every aspect of the life you lead. Even though it is simple, further reflection reveals this as a verse of great depth. May we all find ways in our lives to overcome evil with good, and hopefully make the world better as a result.

Interesting Movie Fact: This verse was used in the movie "Man on Fire", starring Denzel Washington, in a conversation between the main character, Creasey, and a nun. ("Man on Fire" Fox 2004)

The 25th Greatest Bible Verse – Psalm 34:19

#25 – A righteous man may have many troubles, but the LORD delivers him from them all. (Psalm 34:19)

One of the first things to note here, is that it does not say a "righteous man" will NOT have troubles...in fact it says a righteous person will have MANY troubles. Some people mistakenly believe that if you are a good person and do the right thing, you will never have trouble in your life. In fact, many times doing the RIGHT thing in life will lead to more trouble. The point here being that you will face trouble, but it will be okay.

The Bible is letting us know that doing the right thing, while it may not always be easy, surely leads to better things than taking the easy way out does. Wouldn't it be great if governments, politicians, and other leaders around the world were more willing to accept the trouble that comes with doing what is right? Imagine how much better of a chance all of us have at a happy life if we can rest assured that we will always be delivered from our troubles...even if those troubles are many!

Interesting Note: It is believed that this Psalm was written when King David's life was saved.

The 31st Greatest Bible Verse – James 5:13

#31 – Is any one of you in trouble? He should pray. (James 5:13)

Rarely does it get more simple and true than this verse right here. If you are in trouble....pray! Sometimes, actually *many* times in my own life, I have unnecessarily complicated things. Every time I have done this, I made matters worse.

When we are in trouble, praying is taught in the Bible as a natural part of the process of getting out of trouble. The more often we practice the power of prayer, the better we will get at it. It would also seem logical that if we get really good at praying, we can probably prevent a large amount of trouble that would otherwise come our way.

A long time ago when I was still in high school, a teammate of mine lost his temper while we were playing basketball. He lashed out at me physically and managed to cause me to lose my own temper. In a fit of uncontrollable rage, I told him to step outside with me so we could handle this like men. The first thing I am grateful for is that he refused to step outside. It was a Friday afternoon practice, and we would not see each other again until Monday.

I prayed over the weekend about how to handle the situation, and the most amazing thing happened. During the sermon that Sunday, the pastor was preaching about Noah and the ark. Yet, somehow, I distinctly heard the words, "When you are bouncing the ball, turn the other cheek." Those words were crystal clear in my mind as if the pastor had said them, and yet the sermon at that moment was about the animals being chosen two by two. This gift from above inspired me to seek out that guy first thing Monday morning to apologize for my behavior. As it turns out, he was trying to find me to do the same, and that apology allowed us to have a great relationship across several sports for the next couple years.

Funny thing about prayer is that the answers you need can come in ways you never expect. Prayer helped me to avoid trouble and gain a good friend for years after. Next time you find yourself in trouble, give prayer a chance; the results may surprise you.

Related Quote: "Without the assistance of the Divine Being ... I cannot succeed. With that assistance, I cannot fail."

~ Abraham Lincoln

The 26th Greatest Bible Verse – 1 Corinthians 13:13

#26 – And now these three remain: faith, hope, and love. But the greatest of these is love. (1 Corinthians 13:13)

One of my personal all-time favorite little sayings is "Less is More". This verse is living spiritual proof of just how true that saying is. Faith, hope, and love are three of the most important things in life. That the greatest of these is love goes without saying. Sometimes our daily lives get complicated, and we get ourselves into all kinds of trouble with family, friends, work, and more. Getting back to the basics and remembering how powerful faith, hope, and love can and should be in our lives can make a tremendous difference. We need to remember and choose to live accordingly with the knowledge that the greatest of these is love. Saying the words and showing this love every opportunity we get is extremely important, as none of us knows how much time we will have with the people we love. We must be sure to let them know it every chance we can. Have faith that there is a reason for most of the things that happen to us, and hope that the future will continue to be brighter for us all.

Related Movie Quote: From the movie "Gandhi".

Gandhi: "When I despair, I remember that all through history, the way of truth and love has always won. There have been tyrants and murderers, and for a time, they can seem invincible, but in the end, they always fall. Think of it, always."
("Gandhi" Sony Pictures 1982)

The 40th Greatest Bible Verse – Proverbs 3:5-6

#40 – Trust in the Lord with all your heart and lean not on your own understanding; in all ways acknowledge him, and he will make your paths straight. (Proverbs 3:5-6)

At times, it seems to be exceedingly difficult to follow this advice. So often in my life I have received signs of what I should do and ignored them.   I was given messages that were obviously attempting to lead me in the direction I should go, and I did not listen.   As a result, I have had to experience great failure, loss, and mistakes in order to finally follow the advice given from this powerful Bible verse.

When I did finally pay attention, just as it says, my path was made straight, so to speak.   Everything became easier, and my life would almost instantly change for the better.   Take it from me, it is so much better to just trust and acknowledge. Unfortunately for most of us, we have to learn these things the hard way.   Hopefully, reading something like this can help some of us to avoid the difficulty we'd otherwise face.

Related Fact: Faced with his own challenges in his professional career after being cut from his team, NFL Quarterback Tim Tebow tweeted this Bible verse. Tebow made this a great example in real life of someone able to trust and acknowledge God in their life even in the face of adversity.

The 41ˢᵗ Greatest Bible Verse – Hebrews 11:1

#41 – Now faith is being sure of what we hope for and certain of what we do not see. (Hebrews 11:1)

As mentioned earlier, a long time ago, somebody explained to me that you simply cannot have faith and doubt at the same time. Much like we cannot be dry and wet, or a little bit pregnant, faith and doubt are pretty much polar opposites. So, we can logically conclude that having faith also means having zero doubt.

In order for great things to happen to us, we need to master our ability to have faith in things long before they actually happen. This verse is an affirmation of that, and points out that faith is being certain even of what we do not see. Many people have to see things in order to believe them. Funny thing about that is that most of the great successes in world history required faith for many years before anything tangible could be seen. That faith was what resulted in the great success.

Getting rid of our doubts and being able to SEE something long before it is actually visible are both necessary parts of long-term success in just about anything. We must be certain, even if we do not yet see!

Related Quote: "The best and most beautiful things in the world cannot be seen or even touched – they must be felt with the heart." ~ Helen Keller

The 46ᵗʰ Greatest Bible Verse – James 2:26

#46 – As the body without the spirit is dead, so faith without deeds is dead. (James 2:26)

Too many times over the years I have personally run into people who have focused on faith alone. Their thinking being that it doesn't matter what you DO, it only matters whether or not you BELIEVE. This verse right here shows us in no uncertain terms that we cannot just have faith; we must also back it up with action. We need to live our lives in accordance with the faith that we have. This means actually doing the right thing as often as we can, helping out whenever possible, and doing the best we can to set a good example of what living a good life really is.

To ignore this powerful advice from the Bible quite obviously has dire consequences. As a real life example, my wife had a lot of faith that she would be able to beat the disease she was up against. She didn't just sit around though; she took massive action in her attempts to be cured. I will always be able to tell our children she did everything possible to stay with them for as long as she could. In the end, while her body may have died, her spirit lives on, and her many friends and loved ones continue to be inspired not only by the depth of her faith against impossible odds, but the strength of her actions as well.

Related Quote: "Our deeds determine us, as much as we determine our deeds." ~ George Eliot

The 51st Greatest Bible Verse – Hebrews 11:6

#51 – And without faith it is impossible to please God, because anyone who comes to him must believe that he exists and that he rewards those who earnestly seek him. (Hebrews 11:6)

There it is, plain as day. Without faith, it is impossible to please God. This explains so very much doesn't it? Especially when we take into account that faith is something that either we have, or we don't. Too many people seem to be under the false impression that you can have a "little bit" of faith. The truth as previously stated, is we have faith or we do not, there is no in-between. We can see it in our own lives if we are honest with ourselves.

Faith is essentially the absence of doubt, so how many times have we had doubt? For every one of those times we had any doubt, during those same moments we lacked faith. Let's just think about that for a moment; every time we had doubt, we also lacked faith, meaning it was impossible to please God. If our lives are not what we want them to be, is it possible some of the reason might be directly related to this? On the other hand, if we choose to look at the more positive side of this...if we do have faith, and believe, then we will most certainly be rewarded, and every part of our lives can be changed for the better. There is nothing we cannot be, have, or do, if we but believe and earnestly seek God in our lives.

Related Movie Quote: From the movie "Secondhand Lions".

Hub: "Sometimes, the things that may or may not be true are the things that a man needs to believe in the most: that people are basically good; that honor, courage, and virtue mean everything; that power and money, money and power, mean nothing; that good always triumphs over evil; and I want you to remember this, that love, true love, never dies. You remember that, boy. Doesn't matter if they are true or not. A man should believe in those things because those are the things worth believing in."

("Secondhand Lions" Warner Bros. 2003)

The 101st Greatest Bible Verse – Matthew 7:12

#101 – In everything, do to others what you would have them do to you, (Matthew 7:12)

One of the smartest Bible verse breakdowns I heard many years ago involved this verse. What was said was simple yet profound: in the Old Testament, we were essentially given Ten Commandments to follow in order to live life the right way according to God. In the New Testament, Jesus came and simplified everything down to only two rules. 1) Forgive, and 2) Do unto others as you would have them do unto you.

This really is one of the most important Bible verses in existence because it represents half of the new rules we received in the New Testament part of the Bible. Additionally as this book will show, this Bible verse is taught in various ways over and over again throughout the Bible. Basically, it is advice that works for the entire wheel of life, and is incredibly flexible in its ability to help improve the overall quality of a person's life.

Treat people the way you want to be treated, and, for the most part, they will return the favor. This becomes difficult when the other person does not return the favor, or when we don't realize we are not treating people as well as we think. In either case, if we keep working on gaining a better understanding of how to treat people, we will in turn end up with a better life as a direct result.

Interesting Thought: You will notice that this verse is similar to a couple others included in this list of the 101 Greatest Bible Verses. That is the reason why one version of this was chosen as #1. This was such important advice, it had to be given to us in the Bible several different times and several different ways to try and help more people to be able to understand the significance and apply it to their lives. Following this example, we have included more than one in our list and made it the first and the last of the 101 Greatest Bible Verses!

The 82nd Greatest Bible Verse – 2 Corinthians 5:7

#82 – We live by faith, not by sight. (2 Corinthians 5:7)

Hmmm, here we are with another of the little Zen-like statements the Bible makes from time to time. What does this mean? Too often, we need to see the proof of something with our own eyes. It has become too difficult for people to take something on faith; they need to "SEE" it in order to believe it.

Ironically, this runs contrary to virtually anything great that has been accomplished in the history of mankind.   Electricity, airplanes, automobiles, radio, computers, cell phones, antibiotics, and virtually every great invention came about because somebody had faith long before anything could be seen. Great Success Stories like walking on the moon, the civil rights movement, or even America's own independence are like this as well.

People of great vision have the ability to live by faith instead of by sight. Want to live an exceptional life, too? Then first, we must find a way to live by faith instead of sight; it is a fundamental truth that cannot be avoided.   It is also a very necessary component for a truly successful life!

Related Movie Quote: From the movie "Miracle on 34th Street".

Fred Gailey: "Faith is believing when common sense tells you not to."("Miracle on 34th Street" Twentieth Century Fox 1947)

CHAPTER FOUR
"FINANCIAL"

"Financial success, as well as most success in life, is not about perfection, it's about direction."

~ Donald Lynn Frost

The 9th Greatest Bible Verse – Luke 6:38

#9 – Give, and it will be given to you. A good measure, pressed down, shaken together and running over, will be poured into your lap. For with the measure you use, it will be measured to you. (Luke 6:38)

There are very few ways to do a better job of explaining the value of being charitable in this life than this Bible verse. Giving to others should be something that comes naturally for all of us, and yet for many it is a hard thing to do. Too many people are looking for help rather than trying to figure out how to give it.

Point blank, it is a universal law that is more than confirmed here in this Bible verse that the more we give in life, the more we get. This is not the case; however, if the only reason we give is to receive. If we make it a part of our daily life to give as much as we can, then it will come back to us. This is just as real as gravity; it is an absolute law of life, and following it will make all the difference in the world for any of us that are able to do so.

Related Quote: "We make a living by what we get, but we make a life by what we give." ~ Winston Churchill

The 16ᵗʰ Greatest Bible Verse – Proverbs 16:3

#16 – Commit to the Lord whatever you do, and your plans will succeed. (Proverbs 16:3)

Commitment seems to be a thing that most people try to avoid as much as possible in their lives. To make an actual commitment to something requires...well...commitment. Obviously, when we commit to something, it means that we have to follow through and try to make whatever it was we were committing to actually happen.

The hidden beauty in these words of wisdom is the reality that making any kind of commitment in the first place greatly enhances one's ability to succeed. Making that commitment to God, well, imagine how much more magnified that ability to succeed becomes. Hence, the declaration here, straight from the Bible, that if we commit to God in whatever we do, we will succeed.

How can you not love to hear something like that? See, long before somebody wrote, "if you fail to plan...you plan to fail," the Bible brought this valuable lesson, which virtually guarantees our ability to be successful at anything we plan, provided we have made a commitment to God.

Related Quote: "The quality of a person's life is in direct proportion to their commitment to excellence, regardless of their chosen field of endeavor." ~ Vince Lombardi

The 23rd Greatest Bible Verse – 1 Timothy 6:10

#23 – For the LOVE of money is a root of all kinds of evil.
(1 Timothy 6:10)

Few verses from the Bible have been twisted and manipulated more than this one. I have lost count of the times I've heard it said, "Money is the root of all evil". However, leaving out that key word "love" changes everything.

Money is and always has been nothing more than a tool. As with most tools, the power of it being used for good or evil lies completely in the user of that tool. In the hands of the right person, it can be a tool for good. The creation of jobs, the establishment of foundations, the ability to help people truly in need; these are just a few of the things that money in the hands of the right person can do.

In the wrong hands, that same money can be used to oppress, manipulate, dominate, discriminate, and many other negative things. It is incredibly important to remember that the lesson the Bible teaches us is that it is the LOVE of money that is the root of all kinds of evil...not the money itself. Clearly, if we value money over all of the other important aspects of life, we are in for a world of trouble.

On the other hand, realizing that this same money is just a simple tool that can be the root of all kinds of good as well, is an important fundamental truth. Perhaps the greatest value money has is the freedom it can provide us to work on all the things in life that are more important. May none of us ever value money for more than the simple tool that it is, and may we also be able to use it for the greater good whenever possible.

Related Quote: "The highest use of capital is not to make more money, but to make money to do more for the betterment of life." ~ Henry Ford

The 32nd Greatest Bible Verse – Job 22:21

#32 - Submit to God and be at peace with him; in this way prosperity will come to you. (Job 22:21)

Truth be told, this is a verse I have tried to follow with much difficulty. It is not an easy thing to submit to God. Most of us like to think we are in control, myself probably more so than the average person. To submit is something that runs counter-intuitive to what my natural instincts tell me to do.

All I can tell you is what is right there in those words. The moments in life where I have been able to successfully submit to God, prosperity has been virtually boundless in all areas of my life. The times when I did not or when I chose to blatantly disregard, suffice it to say that prosperity disappeared, and rather quickly at that. If we figure out how to do this in our lives we reap not just the prosperity, but the amazing inner peace that comes along with it.

During the final days of my wife Natalia's life, she found this peace in ways one usually only sees in movies. This was all despite the fact that everything she was trying to save her life was not working. Even in the face of many unscrupulous people taking advantage of her condition her peace was unwavering. She virtually glowed with a serenity generally reserved for saints, and people like Gandhi. As the final sands of time trickled through for her in this life, she managed to submit to God and enjoy each last moment in ways that must have brought a smile to God's face. It is my sincerest belief that her ability to follow this Bible Verse in her last days, brought her a different kind of prosperity, the treasure of remaining able to physically live right up until the end. That is a gift the richest people in the world would pay any price for in their own final days. May each of us find a way to submit to God in our own lives, so that we may have the prosperity we need, whatever it may be.

Interesting Movie Fact: In the movie "The Great Debaters", the director and actor Denzel Washington purposefully added a prayer to the beginning. It was not part of the original script, but was a choice he made as the director. (Beliefnet)

("The Great Debaters" The Weinstein Company 2007)

The 27th Greatest Bible Verse – Proverbs 14:23

#27 – All hard work brings a profit, but mere talk leads only to poverty. (Proverbs 14:23)

During elementary school, one of my first coaches taught me that "Luck" was actually spelled "Work". The idea basically being that the harder we worked, the luckier we would get. Along that same idea, here we are with the Bible laying out yet another brilliant verse. This one pointing out that actual hard work is what brings a profit, not merely talking about it. From a business standpoint, this is valuable advice.

Our society has collected dozens of related sayings over the years. A few of these you may have heard of would be "Talk is cheap" or "Actions speak louder than words". Over the years, I have met a lot of people who "Talked the Talk" but never "Walked the Walk" so to speak. For some people, this is a lesson that often takes a lifetime to learn and apply. All of us need to be careful in business and in life to not just talk about what needs to be done. Working hard clearly brings a profit, but equally as important, just talking about what needs to be done leads to poverty. Simple, yet important advice written thousands of years ago that still is every bit as true today!

Related Quote: "There is no substitute for hard work." ~ Thomas A. Edison

The 34ᵗʰ Greatest Bible Verse – 2 Corinthians 9:6

#34 – Remember this: Whoever sows sparingly will also reap sparingly, and whoever sows generously will also reap generously. (2 Corinthians 9:6)

One of the many great things about the Bible is its unique ability to provide amazing analogies that teach life-changing lessons. The comparison of planting seeds (sowing) with what we get out of life is pure genius. In other words, if we do very little to help ourselves, then very little will be received by us. On the other hand, if we go out and do as much as we can, then we can expect big things to come to us. In my life, I have seen far too many people just sitting back, waiting for a better life to happen. Expecting things to get better on their own, sitting around thinking about a better life — with no action — is not going to work out very well. This verse is proof that if we want more, we need to find a way to do more. Far too many people are looking for some kind of shortcut. How does that saying go..."the only place that success comes before work in life....is in the dictionary!"

Related Movie Quote: From the movie "Kingdom of Heaven".

Nasir: "You reap what you sow. You have heard of this, no?" ("Kingdom of Heaven" 20ᵗʰ Century Fox 2004)

The 39th Greatest Bible Verse – Jeremiah 19:11

#39 – I know the plans I have for you declares the Lord, plans to prosper you and not to harm you, plans to give you hope and a future. (Jeremiah 29:11)

Years ago, somebody said to me, "Those who fail to plan....plan to fail." It was one of those little success phrases that sticks with you. Reading this verse always made me feel like I was destined for success if I tried hard enough, because any plans from above had to be better than what I could ever come up with myself.

When my wife died, there were so many questions. She was such a good person, it did not seem fair. Still, to this day, when I see people wasting their lives with drugs and alcohol abuse, or people doing absolutely nothing with the time they have been given, it is difficult to not get angry. It certainly makes one wonder about the "Plan" referenced here.

Ultimately though, in looking back, there were so many miracles that came out of her passing it helps at least a little bit to rationalize losing her. Five different people's lives were saved because of her organ donations alone. Just think about that for a moment. How many people's lives are changed now forever because of that? I have heard it said that if while we are alive we could save even one person's life, then ours becomes a life well-lived.

Most of the time, we cannot fully understand the larger plan, but if we pay attention, it makes sense. The greater good almost always plays out in some way, and in my experience statements like these in the Bible are made with a powerful kind of truth you don't get anywhere else. Sometimes, things happen that we don't think are a part of the plan, but if we trust that there is a reason, eventually it all works out...sometimes in ways we couldn't have even imagined.

Related Quote: "By failing to prepare, you are preparing to fail." ~ Benjamin Franklin

The 38ᵗʰ Greatest Bible Verse – Deuteronomy 15:10

#38 – Give generously to him and do so without a grudging heart; then because of this the LORD your God will bless you in all your work and in everything you put your hand to. (Deuteronomy 15:10)

How many times have we wondered whether or not being generous had any direct impact on our lives? Here is definitive proof that it most assuredly does. Of course, those who are already generous know this. I learned this when I was very young. My parents taught me the value of tithing 10% of whatever money came my way: birthday money, babysitting money, allowance, etc.

Somehow, when I was a kid with no consistent source of income in my life, I ALWAYS managed to have money show up exactly when I needed it. Birthday money, for example, would arrive in the mail three months late, but right at the time I needed some cash for something. Throughout my whole life, the leanest, darkest times have always been the ones in which I strayed from this philosophy. Bottom line is simple....give generously and WE WILL BE BLESSED!

Related Quote: "Joy can be real only if people look upon their life as a service, and have a definite object in life outside themselves and their personal happiness." ~ Leo Tolstoy

The 42ⁿᵈ Greatest Bible Verse – Luke 16:10

#42 – Whoever can be trusted with very little can also be trusted with much, and whoever is dishonest with very little will also be dishonest with much. (Luke 16:10)

Kind of an interesting verse, isn't it? There seems to be a tendency to overlook the little things both positively and negatively with people too often. Many of us have seen real life examples of businesses, governments, and people in general putting big challenges in the hands of people that had previously failed to handle smaller ones. On the other hand, how many times have businesses, governments, and people discounted a positive track record, because it was considered to be too insignificant to be worthy of consideration? My best experiences with this verse have to do with raising my children. If one of my kids has proven they can be trusted to handle small things, then I need to try and give them an opportunity to prove they can be trusted with something bigger. Perhaps they will let me down, but that is part of the learning process for them, anyway. In relationships, if someone is lying about small things...then they will probably lie about big ones as well. It is a nice little guide for us in life to protect ourselves and to open ourselves up to positive things as well.

Related Quote: "It is not only for what we do that we are held responsible, but also for what we do not do."
~ Jean Baptiste Poquelin Molière

The 48th Greatest Bible Verse – Proverbs 10:4

#48 – Lazy hands make a man poor, but diligent hands bring wealth. (Proverbs 10:4)

Yes it is true, we will be hearing more than once from the good old book of Proverbs. In fact, sometime in my early years of Sunday school, they taught us that if we were struggling with something in our lives, the Bible could help. All we needed to do was to visualize in our minds the problem or problems we were facing and then spin the pages of the Bible and stop whenever it felt right. Almost every time, somewhere on one of the pages we open up will be the advice or perspective we "need".

This is often true, because in the middle of the Bible are the books of Proverbs and Psalms. Between the two of them, there is almost always something inspirational and/or instructional that can be applicable to life in many ways. If we are open to it, using the Bible to help with the bigger and smaller troubles life throws at us can set our minds and souls at ease, and often much faster than could happen without the help. This particular verse is more of a "Life" lesson. It also shows that ultimately striving to make something of ourselves is indeed a good thing, while just wasting away doing nothing, is indeed a bad thing.

Related Quote: "Folks who never do any more than they get paid for, never get paid for any more than they do."
~ Elbert Hubbard

The 49ᵗʰ Greatest Bible Verse – Proverbs 22:1

#49 – A good name is more desirable than great riches; to be esteemed is better than silver or gold. (Proverbs 22:1)

This is definitively an "old school" verse, without a doubt. In today's instant society where everyone seems so concerned with getting ahead and not caring about who gets stepped on in the process, this advice is golden. Our reputations are highly important if we plan to do anything significant with our lives. Sacrificing it to make a quick buck or to make things easier on ourselves in the short-term, only makes things worse for us in the long-term. One of the interesting things about this verse is that it is virtually impossible to "buy" a reputation in this life. Thus, the reason it is so incredibly valuable to protect our reputations; once our names have been ruined, it is very difficult to recover what was lost. In the long run, losing a good reputation is seldom worth it.

Related Quote: "Be more concerned with character than reputation. Character is what you are, reputation is what people think you are." ~ John Wooden

The 75ᵗʰ Greatest Bible Verse – Psalm 112:5

#75 – Good will come to him who is generous and lends freely, who conducts his affairs with justice. (Psalm 112:5)

What a great and simple verse! Wouldn't it be nice if our banking system were to follow it? There are several lessons within this Bible verse. The first is to recognize that the Bible encourages us to be generous, and clearly states that good will come to us if we are. However, we have to make sure we connect the "lends freely" statement with the conducting affairs with "justice".

I don't think it means we are supposed to run around lending our money to anyone and everyone. My own interpretation of this is more along the lines of making sure that we are not stingy and miserly. This is not just about money, but also about all the other things that we have to be generous with in life. Some examples would be our love, time, advice, support, and being willing to lend a helping hand when necessary.

The other side of this has to do with what we have lost recently. Both sides of the banking equation have gotten messed up due to a lack of values, and a willingness to bend and even break the rules to our own advantage. Banks no longer make decisions on the character of a person looking to borrow, and many of the people they used to make those kinds of decisions for no longer honor the commitments they make.

Until we are able to regain some sort of equilibrium where people don't take advantage of every loophole they can find to NOT honor their debts...banks will continue to avoid lending freely, because the risk is too great. Additionally, if banks don't find a way to make investments into things that don't always show up on the balance sheet their risks will never lessen. Really though, this verse is about more important things than money.

Somewhat Related Quote: "A bank is a place that will lend you money if you can prove that you don't need it." ~ Bob Hope

The 53rd Greatest Bible Verse – Proverbs 10:22

#53 – The blessing of the Lord brings wealth, and he adds no trouble to it. (Proverbs 10:22)

All of the latest talk about class warfare, about singling out the "wealthy" as the reason for all the problems we are having right now, seems to be skewing the discussion, and removing it from fundamental truths. People, as a general rule, tend to not be inherently good or bad, but usually various shades of grey. Sometimes, we make good decisions that help people, and sometimes we make bad ones that hurt people whether we are wealthy or poor. The Bible states in many places that there are no issues with wealth in and of itself. Any issues that exist have to do directly with the people themselves and the decisions that they make. Life experience has shown me on many occasions that money just makes people more of who they are. Good people are free to be nicer, while not-so-nice people are free to be meaner. The money just heightens the expression of who they are inside. In the end, the Bible says that the blessings of the Lord bring wealth, and he adds no trouble to it...meaning whatever troubles we are dealing with are assuredly of our own making.

Related Quote: "The wealth of man is the number of things which he loves and blesses, which he is loved and blessed by."
~ Thomas Carlyle

The 70ᵗʰ Greatest Bible Verse – Matthew 5:25

#70 – Settle matters quickly with your adversary who is taking you to court. Do it while you are still with him on the way, or he may hand you over to the judge, and the judge may hand you over to the officer, and you may be thrown into prison. (Matthew 5:25)

This verse stands out to me, not because things work today like they did back when it was written, but because of the spirit of the advice given. So much money and time is wasted in this world on lawsuits. Just getting together and talking things over like rational human beings should do anyway can save everyone involved a ton of money, and a ton of heartache. Even when you are 100% right and someone is trying to take advantage of you through the system, usually it is better to come to a settlement and keep things out of court. Once you get to court just like it says here, you never know what the judge and jury will decide. Stranger things have happened, and it is best for all parties involved to avoid going to court if at all possible! This is great advice in a world rife with litigation and frivolous lawsuits. Ironically, many times the best lawyers will give you the same advice and work to resolve things before court as well!

Related Quote: "Let us never negotiate out of fear. But let us never fear to negotiate." ~John F. Kennedy

The 76th Greatest Bible Verse – Ecclesiastes 10:19

#76 – A feast is made for laughter, and wine makes life merry, but money is the answer for everything.
(Ecclesiastes 10:19)

It is difficult for me to not get a huge chuckle out of this one with all the arguments I have heard over the years about money not being important, etc. See, the Bible exists to offer us advice in the truest sense, and many of the greatest lessons it provides are simple, yet profound. The way that the world works for all of us, unfortunately, is that money is more important than it should be. As a result, we can analyze most of the difficulties we run into, and the problem is either solved with money or easier to get through with money than without. My take on this has always been: let's not kid ourselves; it is important, but only in relation to how little of it you have. The less money we have, relative to what we need to survive, the more important it becomes. Two ways to lessen money's importance in our life: 1) Make more of it; 2) Cut our expenses. Figuring out how to do both can quickly lead to a life that is truly "free", which ironically allows for much more feasting, laughter, and merriment.

Related Quote: "You've gotta dance like there's nobody watching, Love like you'll never be hurt, Sing like there's nobody listening, And live like it's heaven on earth."
~ William W. Purkey

The 86ᵗʰ Greatest Bible Verse – Deuteronomy 8:18

#86 – But remember the Lord your God, for it is he who gives you the ability to produce wealth, (Deuteronomy 8:18)

One of the things I like about this verse is that it once again puts to rest the endless debate about success, wealth, and money that always seems to come up with discussions about the Bible, spirituality, and living life the way God intended.. Clearly, if the Bible is referencing to remember that God gives you the ability to produce wealth, then it is an okay thing. Most of the confusion regarding the pursuit of success in life comes from people who are manipulating others for their own gain. Since most people will never become truly successful financially for a variety of reasons, it is decidedly advantageous for anyone looking to easily gain control of the crowd to say you shouldn't pursue wealth anyway. Let's chalk this verse up as one of the potential deterrents to the endless class warfare that has become so pervasive in our society. If we want to pursue success, do so with both the Bible and God's blessing. If we choose not to, then we shouldn't resent those who do. However, let us remember that we have much to be thankful for in this life, including the opportunity to produce wealth...if we want to, and the choice to pursue something different as well.

Related Quote: "That some should be rich, shows that others may become rich, and, hence, is just encouragement to industry and enterprise." ~ Abraham Lincoln

The 95ᵗʰ Greatest Bible Verse – Deuteronomy 30:9

#95 – Then the Lord your God will make you most prosperous in all the work of your hands (Deuteronomy 30:9)

In my lifetime, while I have been blessed to receive a lot of encouragement, still others lined up against me and did their level best to discourage and stop me from pursuing my dreams. Even the worst criticism, however, pales in comparison to this statement right here, straight from the Bible. God saying he will make you prosperous has to be better than any criticism right?

Hopefully, we are able to put more importance on these words then on any negative ones we are hearing in life. Anyone out there working hard at trying to build something, a business, etc., needs to read this and take heart in the knowledge that God is on your side. How powerful is it to know that all the work of your hands will be not just prosperous, but MOST prosperous.

Of course, we must realize that the type of work, how hard we work, and what kind of a job we do must all be taken into consideration. We still need to keep our expectations in line with our efforts. All that being said, it still feels comforting to me to know that this statement exists, and many times in my own life, I have seen it proven true. Hopefully, in the near future, you too will become "prosperous" in all the work of your hands!

Related Quote: "You are never given a wish without also being given the power to make it come true. You may have to work for it, however." ~ Richard David Bach

CHAPTER FIVE
"EMOTIONAL"

"Happiness comes when we stop complaining about the troubles we have, and say thanks to GOD for the troubles we don't have." ~ Unknown

The 11ᵗʰ Greatest Bible Verse – Psalm 23:4

#11 – Even though I walk through the valley of the shadow of death, I will fear no evil, for you are with me; (Psalm 23:4)

There have been more than a couple Hollywood references for this little verse. My childhood recalls this one being preached about more than a few times by various pastors. What I love about this one is that it gives us a strong, calming instruction for when we face the ultimate difficulty that eventually all of us must ...our death. Knowing that even when faced with death we should fear no evil for God is with us sounds pretty good to me.

Sometimes the world that we live in complicates things. Often in our attempts to prolong or save our lives through technology, the fear of death only grows. Witnessing my wife choosing to live her last days without being hooked up to a machine but instead enjoying and savoring each of her last moments because she feared no evil was an unforgettable blessing. This has also guided many of our finest armed service members home safely or ushered them into the next life without the fear that might otherwise have been there. This Bible verse can be a great source of comfort for our families as well as ourselves when reaching the end of our journey on earth.

Related Movies: "Pale Rider" (Warner Bros. 1985) "Rooster Cogburn" (Universal Pictures 1975), "We Were Soldiers" (Paramount Pictures 2001) "Titanic" (Paramount Pictures 1997) just to name a few.

The 35th Greatest Bible Verse – Ephesians 4:26

#35 – Do not let the sun go down while you are still angry. (Ephesians 4:26)

One of the first sermons that I can vividly recall from my childhood was about this Bible verse. I will never forget the pastor's story about two brothers who went to bed angry with each other; something happened to one of them, and they never got the chance to tell each other they were sorry. Maybe the fact that I have a little brother made this a particularly memorable lesson.

My family tries hard to live by this philosophy in our household; and it is real life wisdom at its finest. Many conflicts that last for years between families, friends, and even lovers, could be avoided by simply following this advice. Granted, it isn't easy in the heat of the moment, but if everyone has agreed that they simply cannot go to bed angry with each other, then it makes it possible. This is especially golden advice for families in particular, and incredibly important for the long-term emotional health of almost all relationships in general.

Related Quote: "Anger is an acid that can do more harm to the vessel in which it is stored than to anything on which it is poured." ~ Mark Twain

The 36th Greatest Bible Verse – 1 John 4:16

#36 – And so we know and rely on the love God has for us. God is love. Whoever lives in love lives in God, and God in him. (1 John 4:16)

Isn't it interesting how many verses like this are so simple and profound at the same time within the Bible? Whoever lives in love, lives in God, and God in him! It is a truth that many of us spend our entire lives missing. The daily grind of life can make us forget the simple pleasures of just loving the people around us. If we are able to simply live our lives in love, well, the biggest issues we face in life sort of fade into the background.

When my wife passed away, despite the fact we had lived an incredible life together, the only regrets that I had were the moments when I could have loved her even more. Tiny, but now much more important moments, when I should have stopped whatever I was doing to focus on her. In retrospect, the time I spent away from her trying to find money to save her would have been better spent just being with her. It seems to me that this is true for everyone and everything that we do. When we reach the end of our lives, one of the biggest regrets that all of us face will be the love that we held back while we were here. The Bible is teaching that, finding a way to live this way...is as worthwhile of an endeavor as we will ever take in our lifetime.

Related Movie Quote: One of my favorite films is the little known movie "Always". The main character dies but comes back as a sort of guardian angel. It is a great movie with many memorable moments, but the following quote has always stuck with me. This is Al's last chance to speak to the love of his life on earth before he must leave for heaven.

Al: "I love you, Dorinda. I love you. I should have told you that a long time ago...I should have said the words, because I know now, that the love we hold back is the only pain that follows us here." ("Always" Universal Studios 1989)

The 43ʳᵈ Greatest Bible Verse – Isaiah 41:10

#43 – Do not Fear, for I am with you; (Isaiah 41:10)

I have always been fascinated with adventure stories. Reading Robin Hood, Robinson Crusoe, and Call of the Wild, to cherry pick a few of my early favorites. The best characters in those stories were fearless in the face of overwhelming odds. This lack of fear is what helped them to overcome the impossible.

For a long time, I have felt that one of the reasons we are put here on this earth, is to overcome our own fears. Some of those fears are universal and keep or prevent us from living our lives to their maximum potential. One of the most common is a fear of death. Ironically, this is a fear that quite often prevents people from being able to live their lives to the fullest.

I will never forget my wife Natalia becoming a real life hero when diagnosed with an incurable brain tumor. She managed to live her life better in the face of death, than most of us who get to live out our entire lives will manage to do. She overcame her fears in a big way, and one of the biggest reasons for this was her acceptance of God in her life.

The shortcut to this is found in this verse. If you know and accept in your heart that God is with you, it sure makes it easier to do away with fears that can paralyze many of us in life. There is a wonderful, deep sense of calm that comes over you during difficult times if you can remember this verse. Having witnessed this personally, I hope everyone finds a way to benefit from this great wisdom whenever facing their own fears.

Related Famous Moment: At his inaugural address, during the United States Great Depression, President Franklin D. Roosevelt declared, "The only thing we have to fear is fear itself."

The 44th Greatest Bible Verse – Jeremiah 31:3

#44 – I have loved you with an everlasting love.
(Jeremiah 31:3)

This verse is one of those total feel-good statements that are found throughout the Bible. When you read something like this and realize how amazing it is to be loved with an "everlasting" love, it is pretty hard to not feel great about life in general. I have always felt this was an excellent example of how we should love the people in our lives as well.

When I was dealing with the aftermath of my wife's death, I was forced to intensely re-evaluate about 13 years of my life. Did I love her enough while she was here? Could I have loved her more? During some of the darker moments of this unavoidable deeper introspection into my life, it was an immense comfort to read this verse and know that no matter what mistakes I had made, this statement was true. It also helped to consider that regardless of what I could have done better before she died, I will try harder to live up to this example in the future.

So ultimately, this verse helped me get through a very difficult time, and also has challenged me to be better in the future. There can be no doubt this is a great Bible verse for how we feel about ourselves. Of equal importance, it teaches us how to express love to others. Getting better at that expression of love is of immense importance, since none of us knows how long we will have to share those feelings with the people we love most in our lives.

Interesting Fact: The song "I will Always Love You" made famous by Whitney Houston was actually originally a #1 song by Dolly Parton. In fact, the song hit #1 on three separate occasions across 20 years, making it a kind of real world example of how people in general are big fans of Love that lasts! (Wikipedia)

The 47ᵗʰ Greatest Bible Verse – Jude 1:2

#47 – Mercy, peace and love be yours in abundance.
(Jude 1:2)

Abundance is truly one of the all-time greatest words in human history. By definition it means to have "a great or plentiful amount" or "fullness to overflowing". To be given mercy, peace, and love in abundance is an awesome thing. Many lives would be improved dramatically by an abundance of any one of these. This fullness to overflowing is real, and can be felt once we become open to understanding and accepting it.

One thing I have learned in my own life, is that the more of something we give, the more we receive. It felt great to me personally reading this verse, knowing that this abundance would be mine. However, I instinctively knew this would come from giving these things. Being merciful, peaceful, and loving as much as possible in our lives is the shortcut to having an abundance of each ourselves.

Related Quote: "The sage never tries to store things up. The more he does for others, the more he has. The more he gives to others, the greater his abundance." ~ Lao Tzu

The 52ⁿᵈ Greatest Bible Verse – 2 Timothy 1:7

#52 – For God did not give us a spirit of timidity, but a spirit of power, of love and of self-discipline. (2 Timothy 1:7)

Sometimes, it can be extremely helpful to be reassured by the Bible that we were all given great tools to become something more and better in this life. Knowing that we were given a spirit of power is something that can build us up when facing challenges.

Some people confuse being humble with being weak, but this verse reminds all of us that we have power in this life. The self-discipline part is extremely important, and can be easily forgotten with all the myriad of distractions in this day and age. The love part, of course, most people are aware of, although the danger with the love part is not letting the pain of past relationships take away from the love we give to our present and future ones. To KNOW we were given power, love, and self-discipline, is to KNOW how great our lives can really be.

Related Quote: "With self-discipline, most anything is possible." ~ Theodore Roosevelt

The 55th Greatest Bible Verse – Nehemiah 2:20

#55 – "The God of heaven will give us success."

(Nehemiah 2:20)

It amazes me that a great number of people question whether or not we are supposed to be successful in life and have somehow drawn negative ideas from the Bible regarding success. How is this possible given the sheer number of incredible verses that say we will be successful, have success, etc.? This verse states it clear as day, that the God of heaven will give us success.

If we have ever wondered, doubted, or were concerned with whether or not it was okay to be successful...here is evidence that not only is it okay, but if we have faith, it is assured. Sometimes our definition of success is different than it should be, but make no mistake about it, the Bible tells us over and over again we can, should, and will be successful. If we are having some tough times on the road to our success in life, we must grab a hold of this verse and hang on tight to it. Usually, it is only time and energy keeping us from where we are trying to reach.

Clearly, God, heaven, and the Bible are not the reason for any lack of success in our lives; in fact, they are helping us. Knowing that and believing it may just be the catalyst to get us to the success we are after. Just keep in mind, it is not necessarily instant, but it will be given to us eventually...if we truly earn and deserve it!

Related Quote: "Every great dream begins with a dreamer. Always remember, you have within you the strength, the patience, and the passion to reach for the stars to change the world." ~ Harriet Tubman

The 77ᵗʰ Greatest Bible Verse – Ephesians 4:32

#77 – Be kind and compassionate to one another, forgiving each other, just as Christ God forgave you. (Ephesians 4:32)

What I personally love about this verse is the subtle reminder of our own imperfections. That by far in my own experience is the easiest way to get good at forgiving others...remind yourself of all the times somebody needed to forgive you!

Being kind and compassionate is incredibly difficult for some people, but is a true recipe for happiness in one's life. Learning to forgive people is, of course, an even bigger one. The humongous weight that is lifted for ourselves when we forgive people is almost unequaled. Few things will set you freer in life, yet another reason why this is such good advice.

Related Book Quote: "Those who are at peace with themselves and their immediate surroundings have far fewer serious illnesses than those who are not."

("Love, Medicine & Miracles" by Bernie S. Siegel, M.D.)

The 83rd Greatest Bible Verse – Ecclesiastes 7:9

#83 – Do not be quickly provoked in your spirit, for anger resides in the lap of fools. (Ecclesiastes 7:9)

Seldom have there been truer words to live by. Often times...specifically during rush hour traffic, we get to witness people easily losing their tempers. A good percentage of the accidents that happen are probably a direct result of someone losing their mind over some perceived slight out on the highway. Of course, it happens in other places as well. At sporting events, concerts, even at the grocery store.

Perhaps the most important place for us to never lose our tempers, though, is at home. The best way to teach this lesson to our children is to LIVE it. Setting a good example for our children to live by starts with showing the kind of patience to them that we hope they will show others. There are almost no situations in life where any good comes from being quick to anger. Finding a way to remain calm when our temper is tested brings us much closer to true emotional success.

Related Quote: "It is wise to direct your anger towards problems — not people; to focus your energies on answers — not excuses." ~ William Arthur Ward

The 89th Greatest Bible Verse – 1 Peter 5:7

#89 – Cast all your anxiety on him because he cares for you. (1 Peter 5:7)

I have often wondered how many people in the world are on drugs just because of anxiety, or in simpler terms, worrying. Worrying about things they cannot control...things that according to experts over 90% of the time will never even happen. This verse is one that, if followed, results in reduced stress instantly. Some practical real-world advice that goes right along with this is to not watch the evening news right before going to bed. Stop and think about all the negativity viewed in the average news cast; that same negativity will spin in our minds all night long as we sleep. There is real value in being informed, but it doesn't take a genius to realize that hearing about death, violence, etc. right before going to sleep is probably not good for our health.

One of the great things about having faith is the ability to put all of our troubles and worries into the hands of God. This is in direct contrast to choosing to believe in nothing, which multiplies the stress in one's life in unimaginable ways. Just knowing that a higher power cares for you can help immensely if you allow yourself to believe. Finding a way to do that is better than any Prozac or other prescription drug could ever be. Not to mention the fact the side effects from this are all positive!

Related Book: "Don't Sweat the Small Stuff...and it's all small stuff." ~ Richard Carlson

The 88ᵗʰ Greatest Bible Verse – 3 John 1:11

#88 – Dear friend, do not imitate what is evil but what is good. (3 John 1:11)

As we see throughout the Bible, sometimes the best advice is the simplest. Here we are being told to imitate good....and to NOT imitate evil. Pretty self-explanatory. Many people have a tendency to over-complicate things and often forget the simplicity that can lead to true happiness in life. There is a bit of the "you become who you hang around" type advice here as well.

Understanding that we should imitate good sounds like a pretty good recipe for a better life. Certainly choosing to not imitate evil has to be equally important. Sometimes the best way to learn something, or do something in life is to follow someone else's example. By imitating the lives of people who we know are good, we can easily develop the same traits in our own life and live better as a result.

Related Quote: "For evil to flourish, it only requires good men to do nothing." ~ Simon Wiesenthal

CHAPTER SIX
"MENTAL"

"The measure of intelligence is the ability to change."

~ Albert Einstein

The 5th Greatest Bible Verse – Proverbs 19:20

#5 – Listen to advice and accept instructions; and in the end you will be wise. (Proverbs 19:20)

Sometimes the Bible just straight up reads like the ultimate self-help book. In a lot of ways that is exactly what it is, and can be for anyone open to what it has to teach. Regrettably, all too often, the most powerful, life-altering information happens to be the simplest. That simplicity makes it very difficult for people to see and understand the importance of it. We usually expect things that can have big impacts on our lives to be complicated and difficult.

One of the great lessons of my own life was when a teacher of mine explained to me that intelligent people learned from their own mistakes, but wise people learned from the mistakes of others. To become a student of life is one of the best decisions we can ever make. The beauty of this verse is, of course, that it provides powerful information for becoming a better learner, and gives us the best road map for achieving wisdom within our lifetime, If only more people would listen to advice, and accept instruction, then we would have more wisdom in the world. If we had more wisdom, the world would be a much better place.

Related Quote: "No enemy is worse than bad advice." ~ Sophocles

The 13th Greatest Bible Verse – Mark 9:23

#13 – "If you can?" said Jesus. "Everything is possible for him who believes." (Mark 9:23)

So much has been written by so many different people about the power of positive thinking. It is an accepted fact by many people that what we think has a direct impact on our life. It turns out that a few thousand years ago; the Bible was laying out this same success philosophy for all of us to follow.

One of the best examples of this is what happened to my wife. Despite the fact she had an incurable and untreatable brain tumor, she believed she could beat it. When she was diagnosed, instead of getting depressed, she immediately began racing for a cure. Her belief that she could beat it ended up being one of the most amazing miracles I have ever witnessed in my life. As previously mentioned, the day before she passed away, she was doing a full-on Zumba workout.

When we were in the hospital and she was dying and unconscious the doctors wanted to know how long she had been bedridden. Based on her brain scans, they thought it was impossible when I told them she wasn't bedridden until just then. Even though her disease took her life, it never once beat her. Right up until she spoke her last words, she believed she was getting better. She passed from this world on top; something that according to all the experts was impossible. Her last days were spent running around chasing our children, hiking through forests, riding her bicycle, and so much more. Those last moments, in particular the ones spent with our children, are priceless now. Instead of wasting away in a hospital bed, she was maxing out the joy of her last moments on earth. This Bible verse shows us once again that anything is possible, if we believe!

Related Quote: "Man often becomes what he believes himself to be. If I keep on saying to myself that I cannot do a certain thing, it is possible that I may end up really becoming incapable of doing it. On the contrary, if I have the belief that I can do it, I shall surely acquire the capacity to do it even if I may not have it at the beginning." ~ Mahatma Gandhi

The 14ᵗʰ Greatest Bible Verse – Proverbs 17:27

#14 – A man of knowledge uses words with restraint, and a man of understanding is even-tempered. (Proverbs 17:27)

When looking at an amazing Bible verse like this, one can think of so many examples in our personal lives of this being true. We see even more obvious examples of how true this verse is in the media. The more a person knows, the more they understand about life and other things, the less likely they are to just lose their temper or say silly things.

Most of us can learn from the examples that are set by people actually living out this Bible verse. By attempting to use words with restraint and remain even-tempered, we can one day BE one of these examples for people to follow. Sometimes I think of the chicken or egg dilemma that is discussed so many times....which comes first? Do we develop restraint and even-temperedness by developing our knowledge and understanding? Or does developing restraint and even-temperedness help us to improve our knowledge and understanding? Either way, it is a great verse to reference when deciding how to live our lives.

Related Advice: "If you are patient in a moment of anger, you will escape a hundred days of sorrow." ~ Chinese Proverb

The 21ˢᵗ Greatest Bible Verse – 1 John 4:18

#21 – There is no fear in love. (1 John 4:18)

This is one of the great "tests" of whether or not what you have in a relationship is really love or not. When you really love someone, then you are not afraid, there is no fear whatsoever. You are not worried about what this person is or is not doing...you are only concerned with loving them. This love, if it is real, is all that will matter to you. Should you find yourself with any kind of fear, then what you have is something less than love.

Perhaps this is confusing to some, but love isn't worried about keeping score, it doesn't worry about anything, it just "IS". When you really love someone, all you are concerned with is their happiness and what is best for them. Fear comes from our own insecurities, and there is no room for any of that within real love.

We may, however, realize that loving a particular person is not good for us. This won't come from a fear of not getting equal treatment, it will come as a result of knowing that the way you are loving them is not being returned. When two people understand and love this way, without any fear, that is what we are all meant to experience, and it is the only way to live...and love.

Related Quotes: "Love is what we were born with. Fear is what we learned here." ~ Marianne Williamson

The 59th Greatest Bible Verse – Ephesians 5:15-16

#59 – Be very careful, then, how you live – not as unwise but as wise, making the most of every opportunity (Ephesians 5:15-16)

Here, we have some incredibly sound advice that everyone should follow. Unfortunately many of us take years to get thru living like the "unwise". We party too hard and too often. We don't take the opportunities we are given seriously until it is too late. The advice of making the most of every opportunity is absolutely priceless. In my own personal experience making the most of every opportunity is something everyone should strive to do.

Certainly if we would like to live an above-average lifestyle without many of the financial stresses that bog people down, we must not just learn this lesson...but live it as well. Probably where this verse has the most importance is in the simple daily life decisions. Losing my wife so suddenly and unexpectedly, we didn't have any time to do the things we always wanted to. Luckily for us, we had followed this advice, and as such what was an unavoidably tragic situation became decidedly less, BECAUSE of the way we had already been living our life!

Related Movie Quote: From the movie "Ferris Bueller's Day Off"

Ferris Bueller: "Life moves pretty fast. If you don't stop and look around once in a while, you could miss it."
("Ferris Bueller's Day Off" Paramount Pictures 1986)

The 60th Greatest Bible Verse – Psalm 23:1

#60 - The Lord is my shepherd, I shall lack nothing.
(Psalm 23:1)

As far as popularity of verses from the Bible goes, this has to be one of the ones leaned on by a great many people. My personal take on this verse has always been a positive one. Now, don't get me wrong; I surely don't like to think of myself as a sheep, but the analogy is supposed to be an example of how everything we need is usually there.

We are not always good at recognizing this, and society in general seems to have an awful time being willing to accept that we have what we need. Too much focus goes into wanting more rather than enjoying what we have. The blessing of lacking nothing is a big one, if only we can fully appreciate it. That starts with being grateful for what we have, and where we are, even as we strive to move forward and have more.

Happiness is more about appreciating what we have than it will ever be about getting what we want, and realizing this is a necessary part of recognizing that with God in our lives we lack nothing.

Related Quote: "Be thankful for what you have; you'll end up having more. If you concentrate on what you don't have, you will never, ever have enough." ~ Oprah Winfrey

The 61st Greatest Bible Verse – John 8:12

#61 –When Jesus spoke again to the people, he said, "I am the light of the world. Whoever follows me will never walk in darkness, but will have the light of life."(John 8:12)

Following the Light of the world just doesn't seem like it could ever be a bad thing to me. It is more than obvious, regardless of what anyone may believe, that Jesus was an amazing inspiration and influence on the world we live in. Following the many lessons that he taught would bring the entire world from the darkness it spends far too much time wallowing in.

A verse like this one kind of makes one give a little more respect to all of those "What Would Jesus Do?" t-shirts and bumper stickers that are floating around the world today. If we find a way to heed this advice, then we personally never have to walk in darkness, and that all by itself should be enough incentive to do so. Having the light of life sounds pretty good too!

Interesting Movie Fact: This Bible verse was referenced in the movie "The Shawshank Redemption" during a memorable confrontation between the main character Andy and the Warden. ("The Shawshank Redemption" Warner Bros. 1994)

The 62nd Greatest Bible Verse – Proverbs 26:12

#62 – Do you see a man wise in his own eyes? There is more hope for a fool than for him. (Proverbs 26:12)

This verse actually is part of a personal philosophy that was developed for me years ago by one of the most successful people I have ever worked with. They pointed out to me then, that the dumbest kind of dumb was the person that actually thought they were smart. It resonated with me, and it makes an odd sort of sense, doesn't it? If you think you are really smart, there is a natural tendency to underestimate others...and overestimate yourself, which creates endless opportunity for pitfalls in your life. Now, here is the Bible saying the same thing almost as bluntly, so this pretty much makes it a fact of life in my point of view.

We need to be careful not to overestimate our own wisdom and intelligence, because the true measure of intelligence and wisdom is a willingness to be open and learn. As soon as we think we know it all, we have eliminated the greatest asset of our intelligence...the ability to learn more and more. Following this lesson will ironically automatically give you a huge advantage over those who don't. By not assuming you are the smartest person, you will immediately become smarter...kind of cool, isn't it? Think of it like an instantly-attainable superpower for life!

Related Quote: "The difference between stupidity and genius is that genius has its limits." ~ Albert Einstein

The 63rd Greatest Bible Verse – Psalm 37:4

#63 – Delight yourself in the Lord and he will give you the desires of your heart. (Psalm 37:4)

Lots of people in the world we live in, credit the philosophy of "positive thinking" to success gurus like Norman Vincent Peale, Napoleon Hill, Dale Carnegie, or others. As it turns out, the original teacher of this philosophy was actually the Bible. Amazing isn't it, when you think about it? Basically, be happy with life and God, and you will get everything your heart desires.

Over and over in my life, I have seen people sacrifice their happiness in the chase for something different. When if they could figure out how to be happy in the first place, they would get everything they ever wanted...AND be happy! There are many amazing verses in the Bible—numerous life lessons, and few of them are more important or valuable than this little nugget of goodness.

Related Quote: "The day is what you make it! So why not make it a great one?" ~ Steve Schulte

The 73rd Greatest Bible Verse – Ecclesiastes 5:5

#73 – It is better not to vow than to make a vow and not fulfill it. (Ecclesiastes 5:5)

My dad always taught me for as long as I can remember that our word is our bond. My mom taught me that a promise is something that if you make it, you must keep it. So from a very young age; I learned the importance of this Bible verse. Do not promise to do something if you are not going to do it.

For some reason, most people would rather promise the moon and stars than admit they will not get something done. Too often I have seen people hurt by the careless empty promises people make. Don't do it, ladies and gentlemen...if you cannot make something happen, then by all means, do not make a vow that you will. If you do make a vow, then you better find a way to live up to it. It says so right in the Bible, so don't take it from me, listen to the verse itself. The amount of hurt we cause to people and our reputation by not fulfilling a vow or promise we have made, is difficult to quantify and even harder to repair. Best to never head down that road to begin with!

Related Quote: "You are what you do, not what you say you'll do." ~ Carl Jung

The 90ᵗʰ Greatest Bible Verse – Psalm 29:11

#90 – The Lord gives strength to his people, the Lord blesses his people with peace. (Psalm 29:11)

Two things that most of us can never have enough of in our lives are strength and peace. Strength obviously to be able to get thru the difficult times life throws at all of us. My father raised me to be strong in the face of adversity. Despite spending my whole life developing that strength, I was ill-prepared for the loss of my wife. There were dark times where the only thing that saved me was a strength from above.

The inner peace to be able to be at one with the world we live in seems to be rather elusive for most people. However, if we tap into the blessings we receive from verses like this one, we can speed up and enhance that peace in our lives.

More than once during the early months after my wife's passing; I felt the peace that passes all understanding. The best way I can explain it, is to be filled with an overwhelming sense of calm in your life. It is knowing with every cell in your body that no matter how bad things are, somehow everything is going to be okay. If it weren't for Bible verses like this one, and more importantly, the true strength and peace that we are all blessed with, I am not sure I could have made it through the most difficult moments of my life.

Related Thought: People often say that God will not give us more than we can handle. This is not necessarily true for several reasons. The first being that in my opinion God does not usually cause the bad things in life, evil does. So evil can most certainly overwhelm us, bad things can be far beyond what we are capable of handling...**on our own**, that being the key point. However, with the strength that we get from God, and from empowering ourselves with knowledge and inspiration from the Bible, we can overcome virtually anything no matter how difficult. Realizing this brings the blessing of peace.

The 78th Greatest Bible Verse – Ecclesiastes 11:8

#78 – However many years a man may live, let him enjoy them all. (Ecclesiastes 11:8)

I spent most of my life trying to LIVE this verse. In fact, I probably tried too hard to enjoy some of the years I have spent on planet Earth. However, when my wife passed away, the power of this verse became far more dramatic than it ever had been before. None of us has any idea how many years we are going to get in this beautiful thing called life. My wife only got 34 years and I was blessed to have been with her for almost 13 of them.

Regardless of how many years we get, life is pretty short...so this is just about as good of advice as anyone could ever follow. ENJOY every year you get...cause far too soon it is going to be over and done with, and let's face it...when we are lying on our deathbeds...any year we did not find a way to enjoy, is probably going to be considered a waste.

So make the most of what you get...we owe it to those who have passed on already, cause no matter how wondrous the next life may be...I am pretty sure my wife would have loved to get a few more years with her children. Life moves pretty fast, make sure to slow down long enough once in a while to truly enjoy it!

Related Movie Quote: From the movie "Dead Poets Society".

John Keating: "Carpe diem. Seize the day, boys. Make your lives extraordinary." ("Dead Poets Society" Touchstone Pictures 1989)

The 91ˢᵗ Greatest Bible Verse – Matthew 6:27, 6:34

#91 – Who of you by worrying can add a single hour to his life? (Matthew 6:27) and also, Therefore do not worry about tomorrow, for tomorrow will worry about itself. Each day has enough trouble of its own. (Matthew 6:34)

They say that over 90% of the things that we worry about will never come to fruition. So much time and energy is wasted worrying about things that will never happen. It goes without saying that stress, which leads to so many health issues for people, is usually the result of worrying. So yet again we have the Bible dishing out incredible life altering advice. We can get rid of probably 90% of our stress by following these powerful words. Each day has enough trouble of its own, so don't worry about tomorrow. Easier said than done, but truly words to live by!

Related Movie Quote: From the movie "Seven Years in Tibet".

Dalai Lama: "We have a saying in Tibet: If a problem can be solved, there is no use worrying about it. If it can't be solved, worrying will do no good."

("Seven Years in Tibet" TriStar Pictures 1997)

The 94ᵗʰ Greatest Bible Verse – Ecclesiastes 3:1

#94 – There is a time for everything, and a season for every activity under heaven: (Ecclesiastes 3:1)

When our family was unexpectedly faced with the loss of my wife, it was very difficult to come to grips with the how and the why. These questions of course are the same ones that everyone faces when they lose a loved one...especially if it was unexpected or what we believe to be too soon. There is real value in this verse from Ecclesiastes, because it is the type of wisdom that can keep us grounded during moments like these. The type of moments when we are faced with a loss so great it threatens to swallow us up.

There is a time for everything, and a season for every activity under heaven. All of us will one day be faced with our own mortality. On that day, or in the days before that when we must handle the loss of those we love, this verse provides a simple yet deep comfort. There is a time and a season for everything. It doesn't say we get to choose that time, but it offers up the wisdom of realizing the value of enjoying the time and season we are in.

In a way this is the Bible's way of saying to live in the moment whenever you can. Know that there is of course a time to die for all of us...and a time to live as well. We must enjoy the living part every day that we can so that when we are at our own life's end, we will be filled with a deep sense of calm, and a real feeling of satisfaction at the life we led. My wife Natalia understood this very well, and left a lasting legacy of how to face the end with an amazing passion and enthusiasm for life. May all of us find a way to maximize the time and season we are in...so we will be ready to face the end with the same passion for life we lived with!

Related Movie Quote: From the movie "Gladiator".

Marcus Aurelius: "When a man sees his end, he wants to know there was some purpose to his life."

("Gladiator" Paramount 2000)

The 92nd Greatest Bible Verse – Luke 11:35

#92 – See to it, then, that the light within you is not darkness. (Luke 11:35)

One of the more Zen-type verses, it was chosen for its inherent simplicity. Can any of us imagine what our world would be, if everyone simply made sure that the light within them was not darkness? While this is certainly not the easiest thing to do, it is a strong lesson that rings true on so very many different levels.

Embracing the light within us instead of the darkness turns every aspect of our lives positive rather than negative. Figuring out how to emphasize all that is good instead of giving into to the dark side so to speak makes a huge difference in life. If we find a way to accomplish this mentally, we will quickly find that the light within us shines on every aspect of our lives, not just mental.

Related Quote: "Darkness cannot drive out darkness: only light can do that. Hate cannot drive out hate: only love can do that." ~ Martin Luther King, Jr.

CHAPTER SEVEN
"SOCIAL"

"The only way to have a friend, is to be one."

~ Ralph Waldo Emerson

The 17th Greatest Bible Verse – Romans 12:16

#17 – Live in harmony with one another. Do not be proud, but be willing to associate with people of low position. Do not be conceited. (Romans 12:16)

One of the great early influences on my life was my Grandpa Polk, my mom's father. He was an amazing person...one of the kindest, nicest people I have ever known my entire life. Regrettably he passed away when I was around 6 years old, but not before he taught me some incredibly valuable lessons.

My Grandpa Polk told me when I was about 4 years old, that the reason why my own father was a great man, was that despite the fact my father was incredibly intelligent and well educated, he could just as easily talk to a gas station attendant as the president of a company. He said that my dad would never make anyone that wasn't educated feel bad about it, because he would communicate in a way that made them feel equal. While I didn't fully understand it at the time, it still sounded like something that was a good thing. As a result for my entire life I have tried very hard to communicate with people in ways that make them comfortable.

It turns out that this Bible verse pretty much sums up this little story of how great my dad was. Several of the more successful people in life that I have associated with put this another way. They would say "Never forget where you come from...otherwise you are on your way back." The point is of course that regardless of our station in life, we should treat all people with dignity and respect. Thank you to my Grandpa Polk for teaching me this valuable lesson before he was gone, and thank you to my father for living this example his whole life.

Related Quote: "To effectively communicate, we must realize that we are all different in the way we perceive the world and use this understanding as a guide to our communication with others." ~ Anthony Robbins

The 54th Greatest Bible Verse – Psalm 41:1-3

#54 – Blessed is he who has regard for the weak; the Lord delivers him in times of trouble. The Lord will protect him and preserve his life; He will bless him in the land and not surrender him to the desire of his foes. The Lord will sustain him on his sickbed and restore him from his bed of illness. (Psalm 41: 1-3)

Never in my entire life have I been able to understand how and why people bully people that are smaller or weaker than they are. Perhaps it is because I was raised to look out for the little people of the world, to stick up for people who are unable to stick up for themselves. When I was a kid, my father told me several stories about sticking up for people when he was in school. As long as he was around, he simply never tolerated anybody bullying someone...especially people who couldn't defend themselves. So when I stumbled across this little gem of wisdom from the Bible, it was natural that it would become one of my favorites.

Whenever I have been able to in my life, I have tried to stick up for people less fortunate than myself. This verse from the Bible pretty much lays out there all the good karma that comes our way for sticking up for people who need it. It is quite a list...delivers us in times of trouble...protects and preserves our life....blesses us in the land....does not surrender us to our foes....sustains us on our sickbed, and even restores us from illness. Not too many Christmas lists I can think of that would top that. The words in this powerful verse have rung true for me so far in my own life....sticking up for the weak is something more people should do. It is a worthy thing that, according to the Bible, is rewarded!

Related Movie Quote: From the original "The Karate Kid" movie released back in 1984, and a pretty decent anti-bullying movie in its own right.

Daniel: "When do I learn how to punch?"

Mr. Miyagi: "Better learn balance. Balance is key. Balance good, karate good. Everything good. Balance bad, better pack up, go home. Understand?" ("The Karate Kid" Columbia Pictures 1984)

The Number 1 Greatest Bible Verse – Mark 12:31

#1 – "Love your neighbor as yourself." (Mark 12:31)

This is one of the two most important lessons taught throughout the Bible. This entire book could be written about just this one verse. It is the single greatest lesson in the history of the world with regards to dealing with people successfully. If we treat people the same way we want to be treated, if we love people the same way we love ourselves, then we simply cannot go wrong.

The simplest platform, with which one could ever build a truly successful and immensely happy life, is to follow this advice. We made it the number one verse because it is the most versatile of all the verses with regards to living your life. This advice helps your family, friendships, work, business, relationships, etc. If the only thing any of us ever learned from the Bible was this piece of advice, we would be so much the better for it, words cannot adequately describe. Just try LIVING this for a short time and you will be amazed!

Related Quote: "The time is always right, to do what is right."
~ Martin Luther King, Jr.

The 50th Greatest Bible Verse – Leviticus 19:18

#50 – Do not seek revenge or bear a grudge against one of your people, but love your neighbor as yourself. (Leviticus 19:18)

Well, there you have it folks, right there in the Bible, it says to not seek revenge. This is in the Old Testament too, which makes it even more interesting. How many times have we witnessed nations, politicians, businesses, and people ignore these words of advice and destroy their lives and the lives of others seeking revenge?

About the only place this can have even a remote exception might possibly be in sports. Even there though, if your focus becomes all about revenge...then you will most likely get taken out by somebody else you weren't watching or focusing on. It has been said that revenge is a fuel that can only get you so far, and with devastating consequences to both you and your adversary anyways.

Loving our neighbors as ourselves is just good advice. Not bearing a grudge, well sometimes that can be a hard thing to do, but it is definitively something that we should be working on. It is interesting that the love your neighbor advice appears in more than one place in the Bible...must be pretty important right?

Related Quotes: "In taking revenge, a man is but even with his enemy; but in passing it over, he is superior." ~ Francis Bacon

The 57th Greatest Bible Verse – Proverbs 28:27

#57 – He who gives to the poor will lack nothing, but he who closes his eyes to them receives many curses. (Proverbs 28:27)

Well, there you have it! Right here in the Bible we have proof that we need to help the poor. In fact, one could argue that this is a definitive outright command to help the poor or face dire consequences. Too often in life, it is easy to ignore those that are less fortunate than us. Many times we will be unaware of people struggling. What this message is saying is that when we do become aware of somebody in need, if we can, we need to help out.

Finding out that somebody is in need of assistance and then ignoring the situation is a bad move. Not just because it leaves somebody we could help still in a rough spot, but also because it avoiding many curses has to be a good thing to do as well. So the next time you see someone in need, if you are in a position to do something about it, by all means, do what you can. Even if it is a small thing that you can do, clearly every little bit counts!

Related Quote: "Act as if what you do makes a difference. It does." ~ William James

The 58ᵗʰ Greatest Bible Verse – Ephesians 5:1-2

#58 – Be imitators of God, therefore, as dearly loved children and live a life of love (Ephesians 5:1-2)

This has to be one of the hardest lessons that the Bible teaches us. To attempt to imitate God is an incredibly difficult task, and one that most of us can only attempt with scant hope to pull it off. However, putting an emphasis on love in our lives is always a good thing. To live a life of love is something we should all seek to do, and our lives would be so much more if only we could.

I would venture to say that in the final days of my wife Natalia's life she had mastered this. Despite headaches that were constantly causing her intense pain, she somehow exuded nothing but pure love. She touched everyone around her in amazing ways, because they could feel this powerful love emanating from inside her. I will remember this for as long as I live, and hope that one day I can imitate God the way she was able to, even if only for a little while. The happiness that surrounds you because of this, even in the face of death is truly a wondrous thing.

Related Movie Quote: From "E.T. The Extra-Terrestrial".

Elliott: "You could be happy here. I could take care of you. I wouldn't let anybody hurt you. We could grow up together, E.T." ("E.T., The Extra-Terrestrial" Universal Pictures 1982)

The 69th Greatest Bible Verse – Philippians 2:4

#69 – Each of you should look not only to your own interests, but also to the interests of others. (Philippians 2:4)

One of the things that we love about all of these Bible verses is that you can take the verses and interpret them so many different ways. Each of us can look at these verses and contemplate them and how they can help our own lives. It doesn't matter if you agree with my interpretations; the real power is in making your own interpretation that works for you, and that is the real genius in all of this anyway.

The fact that the Bible tells us we should not just look out for ourselves but others as well should come as no surprise. This is a recipe for a happy, successful life. Of course we must look out for ourselves, but in looking out for others as well is where true happiness and satisfaction really comes from. On a basic level, there is no doubt I have enjoyed the times when I bought myself a present, but not nearly as much as when I was able to do something great for someone else. Looking out for others is an essential part of living a truly happy and fulfilled life.

I have thought a lot about how my wife had so much peace when facing death. She spent most of her life looking out for others. She took care of her family back in Russia and watched over her mother here in the United States. She found a way to bring her sister's family to America. So many things she did for others, more by the age of 34 than most will do for others in a lifetime.

She faced her end comforted in the knowledge she had done everything she could in this life for others. May we be even half as generous with our own lives, and we will be blessed.

An Appropriate Quote: "Do all the good you can, By all the means you can, In all the ways you can, In all the places you can, At all the times you can, To all the people you can, As long as ever you can." ~ John Wesley

The 72nd Greatest Bible Verse – Proverbs 3:27

#72 – Do not withhold good from those who deserve it, when it is in your power to act. (Proverbs 3:27)

This is a classic statement that has so much truth to it. We should never withhold good from those who deserve it...especially when it is in our power to act. While at the moment it is difficult to imagine a scenario where I personally would attempt to withhold good from someone, it is great to have this laid out as words to live by.

The two biggest areas in life that come to mind would be with our spouse and children. For some reason, there is often a tendency after being in a relationship for a long time to withhold our affections, compliments, and praise. To try and overcome this, my personal goal when I was married to Natalia was to pay her a minimum of 10 compliments a day. Too many times I failed in the attempt to achieve this; however, trying to hit this every day made sure I at least had some positive words for her.

I also went out of my way to make sure that my "nicknames" for her were positive. For example, I used to call her "Hollywood" because her beauty rivaled that of the top actresses. With my long-term goal being to make movies, I used to joke around that at least I had my own private Hollywood movie being made with her. Despite these efforts, all too often, I held back. Many of us do the same thing with our children.

For years, I have tried hard to whisper words of power and encouragement to my children every night before they sleep. Not sure if this makes up for the many times when I am overly critical in my attempts to teach them, but at least it keeps the thought of not withholding good in my mind. On a larger scale, it is important for us to remember how many people in the world we can help with relatively small commitments. Our family supports a family in Africa for $1 a day. Still, we could and should be doing more. This verse is a great reminder and true words to live by in creating a much happier life not just for ourselves, but our families as well.

Related Quote: "Treat people as if they were what they ought to be and you help them to become what they are capable of being." ~ Johann Wolfgang von Goethe

The 65th Greatest Bible Verse – Ecclesiastes 4:10

#65 – If one falls down, his friend can help him up. But pity the man who falls and has no one to help him up! (Ecclesiastes 4:10)

Boy oh boy, isn't that the truth! Some people do not find out the wisdom in this verse until they have wrecked far too many relationships in their lives. An even simpler way to look at this, is what do you do when a friend asks you to drive them to the airport? When somebody asks you to help them move, what is your response? Are you the person people would call if they had a flat tire in the middle of the night?

Leave it to the good book to give us some more Zen-like advice on friendship. Following it starts with being the person that is there to help a friend up...be there for enough people and you will never have to worry whether or not somebody will be there for you!

Related Quote: "Successful people are always looking for opportunities to help others. Unsuccessful people are always asking, 'What's in it for me?' ~ Brian Tracy

The 71ˢᵗ Greatest Bible Verse – Titus 3:10

#71 – Warn a divisive person once, and then warn him a second time. After that, have nothing to do with him. (Titus 3:10)

This is a particularly difficult piece of advice for most people to follow. Most of us have a relative, neighbor, co-worker, or friend that likes to argue etc. These people cause an immense amount of stress to us in our lives, but because so many of us have a fear of confrontation, we usually just put up with it. The reality is that if somebody really cares about you, and is worth being in your life, then what you think and feel should matter.

The two chances advised here is probably a really good rule of thumb, although if it is a relative you will have to deal with them at holidays and family functions regardless. The point is to not have anything to do with them when you can avoid it. We must give people a chance to not act in a way that is offensive, but if they refuse to change then it is definitively time to move on. Truly words to live by!

Related Quote: "Learning to say 'we feel differently', instead of 'you're wrong', shows real love for our fellow human beings." ~ W.J. Vincent II

The 74ᵗʰ Greatest Bible Verse – Titus 3:2

#74 – to slander no one, to be peaceable and considerate, and to show true humility toward all men. (Titus 3:2)

So here we are once again, with the Bible teaching us lessons thousands of years before others do. My mom and dad taught me that if you don't have anything good to say about someone, then don't say anything at all. This advice is absolutely priceless, unless you are looking for your 15 minutes of fame at all costs. You might be able to get a little bit of publicity now and then, by going off on someone, but you can definitely build a more satisfying career and certainly a better life, around following this Bible verse's advice.

Humility is another thing sorely lacking in today's society. The brashest loudmouths in the world want to be around the most considerate and humble people. It is an unfortunate reality nowadays that people enjoy being entertained by people acting in ways none of us would ever actually tolerate in real life. It is a pity, because many in the younger generations are falling into the trap of actually believing these terrible actions on television are in some way good business or an actual strategy to follow. My thoughts are that for every one person this opposite of the Bible's advice strategy works for, there are at least ten thousand that are ruined because of it. Let's all try to follow this great advice!

Related Quote: "Humility is not thinking less of yourself, it's thinking of yourself less." ~ C.S. Lewis

The 79ᵗʰ Greatest Bible Verse – Proverbs 22:24-25

#79 – Do not make friends with a hot-tempered man, do not associate with one easily angered, or you may learn his ways and get yourself ensnared. (Proverbs 22:24-25)

All of us know at least one person with a "Hot Head" personality. The reverberations of their temper are felt on so many different levels. They can take a small, insignificant situation and blow it into something beyond what it ever should have been. They cause a huge amount of stress to everyone around them, and repeatedly do things that they regret. It is best to stay away from people like this, because whatever their good traits may be, they will always be overshadowed by the temper simmering underneath.

Sometimes the damage that is caused by these tempers cannot be undone. It is hard to measure the amount of emotional damage done to people, and in particular children when they suffer the wrath of someone who loses their temper. Some examples that come to mind are people who are susceptible to "road rage", or freaking out over a child spilling their milk. As an added thought, this Bible verse is reminding us of the well-known advice which is that we become who we hang around. These words are great advice to follow for a happier and safer life.

Related Quote: "Anger dwells only in the bosom of fools."

~ Albert Einstein

The 80th Greatest Bible Verse – Luke 5:39

#80 – And no one after drinking old wine wants the new, for he says, "The old is better." (Luke 5:39)

Okay, so this one might get me in a little bit of trouble with some people, but am going to share it anyway. To me, as this was pretty much a quote directly from Jesus, this is a statement about enjoying life and living a little bit. Too often in my experience, people get caught up in trying so hard to follow "rules" that they miss so much of what life has to offer.

Don't get me wrong, I am by no means advocating excess in any way, but it seems pretty obvious here that there is an appreciation for aged wine. It is a direct acknowledgement that it is okay to enjoy and partake in some of the best that life has to offer. We should all keep in mind, that there are many wonderful things to experience and enjoy in this life that are truly gifts that should be fully appreciated.

Related Quote: "Better is old wine than new, and old friends like-wise." ~ Charles Kingsley

The 84th Greatest Bible Verse – Matthew 7:1

#84 – Do not judge, or you too will be judged. (Matthew 7:1)

Sometimes, when reading these wonderful nuggets of wisdom, it seems to me that most people are living their lives exactly opposite of how they should be. This has been one of the cornerstone philosophies of my entire life, and I still struggle with it on a daily basis. Perhaps one day, with continued effort, I will personally be able to do a better job not judging people.

It is extremely difficult for most of us to see things from another's point of view rather than our own. The Bible, in yet another moment of brilliance, has simplified it for us to easily understand. Do not judge others or you will be judged. That is more than enough incentive for me to try hard not to.

Related Movie Quote: From the movie "Empire Strikes Back".

Yoda: "Size matters not. Judge me by my size do you? Hmm?"

For those unfamiliar, Yoda is only a couple of feet tall, but is one of the most powerful beings in the universe that the "Star Wars" movies are based in. This gives us a very nice example of how dangerous it can be to make judgments about people.

("The Empire Strikes Back" 20th Century Fox 1980)

The 85th Greatest Bible Verse – Ecclesiastes 3:12

#85 – I know that there is nothing better for men than to be happy and do good while they live. (Ecclesiastes 3:12)

For centuries, people have wondered whether or not it was important to do good in this life. Philosophers have on countless occasions debated the value of happiness. To be certain, an endless stream of commercials seeks to sell us that the secret to happiness is whatever it is they are selling.

Here it is, in the simplest of terms, for all to read. There is NOTHING better for men than to be happy and do good while they live. These are pretty strong words coming from the definitive source book on good and evil. For sure, it should matter more what the Bible says to us than some random commercial we caught in the middle of a bleary-eyed internet or television marathon.

So yes, we should take our happiness into consideration when we make both big and small decisions in life. We should also make certain we do as much good as we can...for nothing is better while we live!

Related Movie Quote: From the movie "Steel Magnolias".

Shelby: "I would rather have thirty minutes of wonderful than a lifetime of nothing special." ("Steel Magnolias" TriStar Pictures 1989)

The 96th Greatest Bible Verse – Acts 20:35

#96 – In everything I did, I showed you that by this kind of hard work we must help the weak, remembering the words the Lord Jesus himself said: "It is more blessed to give than to receive." (Acts 20:35)

There are so many ways that I have been blessed in my life. This particular lesson was taught to me many times as a child and has formed a strong foundation for me in life. Far too few people learn this incredibly valuable lesson. Once the amazing energy you feel when you give someone something, or really help someone has touched you, it is something that is felt deep within one's soul.

There will always be people in life that we can help. Occasionally we may be the person that needs help. Sometimes in giving to or helping someone, we find that we actually get as much or more in return.

Related Movie Quote: From the movie "The Bucket List".

Carter Chambers: "Have you found joy in your life? Has your life brought joy to others?" ("The Bucket List" Warner Bros. 2007)

The 93rd Greatest Bible Verse – Exodus 23:8

#93 – Do not accept a bribe, for a bribe blinds those who see and twists the words of the righteous. (Exodus 23:8)

Seems like this has been a big part of a large number of movies, television shows, books, etc. hasn't it? The illicit bribe that changes the storyline...so it should come as no surprise that the Bible advises against accepting this sort of thing.

Surely there are plenty of people who will try and justify why in certain circumstances it is okay to accept a bribe. Chief among them will be the "everyone is doing it" commentary that none of our parents were supposed to let us get away with when we were children. The other being "if I don't accept this bribe, somebody else will, so I may as well benefit."

This type of thinking is a lot of what is wrong with the world nowadays. We think that just because nobody is getting hurt...or we THINK nobody is getting hurt, it should be okay. This is the decidedly large "gray" area of life that is a long, slippery slope. Better to simply follow the advice from the Bible and just avoid this situation.

See, once you accept a bribe, you give away all possibility of being objective, and as it says in the verse, you lose the ability to see. If we have any kind of goal to do the right thing in this life, then accepting bribes is just not something we can ever do, because like a lot of things that slant toward the negative, where will it actually stop?

Related Quote: "The American Republic will endure until the day Congress discovers that it can bribe the public with the public's money." ~ Alexis de Tocqueville

The 97th Greatest Bible Verse – Proverbs 11:12

#97 – A man who lacks judgment derides his neighbor, but a man of understanding holds his tongue. (Proverbs 11:12)

Ah yes, if only people around the world would listen to this golden piece of advice. In fact, how many fights, feuds, arguments, and general all around bad times have been started from somebody mocking, insulting, and putting someone down unnecessarily. Somewhere back in time I was taught to never make fun of people. While that advice was given to me some 20 or 30 years ago, it turns out the Bible was giving out this advice some 2,000 years ago or more. If only the world listened to this advice, what a much better place it would be!

Related Quote: "It is nice to be important, but it's more important to be nice." ~ John Templeton

The 99ᵗʰ Greatest Bible Verse – Exodus 23:9

#99 – Do not oppress an alien; (Exodus 23:9)

Interesting to find this verse with all of the back and forth we hear these days about immigration. This is a topic near and dear to my own heart, with my dearly departed wife having been an immigrant to the United States. Too often, we are quick to judge groups of people we really know little about. Everyone in the United States is a descendant at some point from an immigrant...with the exception of our Native American Indians. This means that the oppression of our immigrants is in fact oppression against the very heritage that made this land great. Of course, there are challenges we need to address, but one of the greatest books ever written says quite simply to not oppress. This seems like good advice to follow—not just for individuals, but far more importantly, for our nation.

Related Poem Excerpt: From the Statue of Liberty…

"Give me your tired, your poor,
Your huddled masses yearning to breathe free,
The wretched refuse of your teeming shore.
Send these, the homeless, tempest-tost to me,
I lift my lamp beside the golden door!"

CHAPTER EIGHT
"FAMILY"

"Home is people. Not a place. If you go back there after the people are gone, then all you can see is what is not there anymore." ~ Robin Hobb

The 8th Greatest Bible Verse – John 3:16

#8 – For God so loved the world that he gave his one and only son that whoever believes in him shall not perish but have eternal life. (John 3:16)

This Bible verse has always created mixed emotions for me. Ultimately, it has to be considered one of the all-time greats because of the huge sacrifice of love it represents. Assuming there is some kind of metaphysical or spiritual laws that necessitated this sacrificing, it is an amazing statement. To give up one's child for the benefit of the entire world....wow, I mean, think about it. As a parent, it is unimaginable to me. So for the Bible to tell us that there is that much love for the world we live in absolutely has to be not just a good thing, but a great thing, for all of us. I have found that not thinking too deep on this one leads to the best feelings about it. Getting a shot at eternal life is not too shabby of an outcome, either.

Interesting Note: The famous football player Tim Tebow wore this Bible verse in eye black during the 2009 BCS Championship Game. More attention was brought to this powerful Bible verse January 8, 2012 when in dramatic fashion, the Tim Tebow led the Denver Broncos defeated the Pittsburgh Steelers in overtime during a playoff game, completing 316 yards, averaging 31.6 yards per pass, and seeing the opposing quarterback throw the only interception of the game on a 3rd and 16 play. (Wikipedia)

The 3rd Greatest Bible Verse – 1 Corinthians 13:4-8

#3 – Love is patient, love is kind. It does not envy, it does not boast, it is not proud. It is not rude, it is not self-seeking, it is not easily angered, it keeps no record of wrongs. Love does not delight in evil but rejoices with the truth. It always protects, always trusts, always hopes, always perseveres. Love never fails. (1 Corinthians 13:4-8)

It has been my experience that most people haven't got much of a clue what love is really all about. Over the years, people have shown this in their actions, and even more have said things to prove it. Most people's definition of love has to do everything with themselves. The truth is, as it says in this most powerful verse, it is not supposed to be self-seeking.

The great masses of people who think they have loved are missing huge chunks of patience, have far too much jealousy, are too easily angered, and keep a laundry list of "wrongs" within a relationship. Figuring out how to love the way this incredibly important verse teaches us to is a lifelong journey for most of us. When we have even just begun to understand the power of this verse, we will no longer be worried about ourselves, but have found the freedom that truly loving gives us all. For when we are more concerned about the happiness of someone we love, then we are happiest when making them happy.

This is the highest definition of love for all of us to aspire to. Figuring out how to live this verse may be the most important thing any of us can do in our lifetime.

Related "Life" Philosophy: Ask anyone if they believe a healthy relationship with regards to true love is supposed to be 50/50 and almost everyone will say yes, absolutely. However, this is actually incorrect, a true love relationship is supposed to be 100/100 with both partners giving 100% all the time and not worrying about whether or not it is equal. This philosophy has guided me to very happy relationships despite my failings, but my wife Natalia was a true master and actually LIVED the 100%.

The 12ᵗʰ Greatest Bible Verse – 1 John 3:18

#12 – Dear children, let us not love with word or tongue but with actions and in truth (1 John 3:18)

So here is a "life" philosophy that I had been given in many different ways, from many different gurus, coaches, and mentors. I never realized it was originally from a Bible verse. In other words, yet again the Bible shows us that so much of the greatest wisdom and lessons for life were originally inspired by this great book.

There are a lot of relationships that would have been saved or ended up totally different if the people involved simply followed this incredibly sound advice. A long time ago, one of my mentors and coaches taught me to watch what people do....not what they say. It was a valuable lesson to learn not just for other people, but myself. This verse teaches us that more important than what we say with regards to love, is what we do with love.

It is not enough to tell people you love them, although that is nice. We have to back it up in actions and deeds. We have to actually live our lives in accordance with this love in order for it to be real and true. I consider myself to be truly lucky that I learned this lesson early in life.

My time with my wife ended up being only 13 years, but because we lived our lives as this verse suggests, my regrets are very few. One of the best gifts she ever gave me was a short while before she was diagnosed with her brain tumor. She took the time to write a list of the 100 reasons why I was a great person. Can you imagine how important that list is to me now? So many people lose their loved ones before they tell them how they really feel. They spend the rest of their lives wondering how that person really felt about them. I will always be eternally grateful that my amazing wife took the time to express so many wonderful thoughts about how she felt about me and our life together. Even now, she is still showing me how to live by this Bible verse. Here's to each of us in love backing up that love with actual deeds rather than just talk, especially with our family, because we never know when it will be too late.

Related Quote: "Love and desire are the spirit's wings to great deeds." ~ Johann Wolfgang von Goethe

The 22nd Greatest Bible Verse – Philippians 2:14

#22 – Do everything without complaining or arguing. (Philippians 2:14)

So it turns out that all that talk from my parents about not complaining was actually a verse from the Bible! Can you imagine? Now many may wonder what the big deal is, especially if we are the type of person to complain all the time or one who loves to argue. This advice reads like something straight out of some of the most powerful self-help books written in history.

When we complain about something, it accentuates the negative aspects of whatever it is; hence, it makes it more negative. When we argue with people, we prevent any opportunity for resolution. There is a distinct difference between arguing and discussing things. One is particularly combative, and the other is not. Essentially, this is advice to create a happier, more positive life. Don't believe it? Try it out for a couple weeks; you might be surprised how much better you feel!

Related Quote: "Do not listen to those who weep and complain, for their disease is contagious." ~ Og Mandino

The 56ᵗʰ Greatest Bible Verse – Luke 11:17

#56 – Jesus knew their thoughts and said to them; "Any kingdom divided against itself will be ruined, and a house divided against itself will fall." (Luke 11:17)

How many times do we see this play out in front of our eyes each year in sports, entertainment, and politics? It is particularly easy to see during championship runs, playoffs, and anytime there is a big moment; we can see that whenever there is division bad things happen. By the same token, whenever there is true teamwork and a willingness to sacrifice for the good of the group, good things happen.

The advice in the Bible can be so obvious and its truth can be life-changing if we would only apply it into our daily lives. More and more we see this one unfortunately within families where instead of looking out for each other, individual family members are looking out for themselves. Suffice it to say, this is NOT the road to happiness, enlightenment, or anything remotely resembling a good life. On the other hand, heeding this advice can provide happiness and contentment that being a part of something greater than ourselves has always given.

Related Quote: "What can you do to promote world peace? Go home and love your family." ~ Mother Theresa

The 66th Greatest Bible Verse – 1 Peter 4:8

#66 – Above all, love each other deeply, because love covers over a multitude of sins. (1 Peter 4:8)

When I first read this verse, it was one of those moments where you really feel something deep, something bigger than yourself. In my life, the love of a great woman proved this time and time again. My wife showed me over and over how true this statement was. The deep love she had for me certainly covered up a multitude of my own sins and mistakes.

Now, during the darkest time of my life, reeling from the kind of loss that can break you, reading this verse again brings a kind of comfort that is almost life-saving in its power. See, this verse assures me that no matter what, everything is okay. Since there was deep love between us; all the mistakes, all the things that could have been done better, simply do not matter. If you can find a way to live this verse, you will have shielded yourself from even life's greatest disasters. Love each other deeply, in all your relationships, not just romantic ones...and it will cover a multitude of mistakes!

Related Movie Quote: From the movie "Meet Joe Black".

Joe Black: "Take love, multiply it by infinity, and take it to the depths of forever...and you still have only a glimpse of how I feel for you." ("Meet Joe Black" Universal Pictures 1998)

The 67ᵗʰ Greatest Bible Verse – 1 Timothy 5:8

#67 – If anyone does not provide for his relatives, and especially for his immediate family, he has denied the faith and is worse than an unbeliever. (1 Timothy 5:8)

As I have pointed out many times in this book, my parents taught me a lot of great things while I was growing up. The importance of family and taking responsibility for the people you love in this life were among the great lessons they gave me. If anyone out there doubts the importance of taking care of your family, this verse clearly demonstrates that it should be a fundamental part of the life we live.

Taking care of our immediate family is of great importance. If more people followed this philosophy, there would be fewer people in need of help. For those of you who are doing the best you can and struggling because of the help you are giving, rest assured that you are doing the right thing. Not only that, but by taking care of your immediate family, you are making sure you will be taken care of as well. In this life and the next!!

Related Quote: "A man should never neglect his family for business." ~ Walt Disney

The 87th Greatest Bible Verse – Proverbs 21:9

#87 – Better to live on a corner of the roof than share a house with a quarrelsome wife. (Proverbs 21:9)

It is truly amazing with this being the first time I have sat down to write since my beloved wife passed away suddenly and unexpectedly....that this would be the verse I would come to. Often times the absolute best advice in the Bible, is the obvious stuff. I was with my wife for a blissful 13 years. She was one of the most amazing people I have ever known. Even on the rare occasion that we did get into an argument about something, she always found a way to calm everything down. Too often, a spouse stokes the fires of an argument instead, which is really what this verse is referring to.

It doesn't have to be just a quarrelsome wife....it could just as easily be a quarrelsome husband causing issues as well. The Bible has words of wisdom and comfort for even the darkest times of our lives. It will be one of my goals to try and write a little bit about these wonderful verses every day moving forward, for no doubt these amazing words of wisdom and sage advice will help me to get through what has become my own personal darkest hour. Heed this advice—be sure to marry someone who is NOT quarrelsome—and your life will be immeasurably happier... beyond words and beyond what most people who do not follow this advice will ever get to experience.

Related Famous Thoughts: "I have always considered marriage as the most interesting event of one's life, the foundation of happiness or misery." ~ George Washington in a letter in 1785

The 100th Greatest Bible Verse – Ephesians 4:29

#100 – Do not let any unwholesome talk come out of your mouths, but only what is helpful for building others up according to their needs, that it may benefit those who listen. (Ephesians 4:29)

It is truly amazing to me how the Bible never stops teaching its willing students. Throughout the process of researching and writing this book, I continue to learn new, wonderful things from the Bible. This verse right here is a brilliant example. A good friend of mine happened to mention it one day, and it was immediately obvious this verse was easily one of the 101 Greatest Verses from the Bible.

There is an entire industry that has basically evolved around teaching people this valuable lesson. How many times in my lifetime, especially growing up did I hear things like, "Sticks and Stones may break my bones, but names will never hurt me"? Or on how many different occasions was I told if you don't have anything good to say, then don't say anything at all? I guess I can count myself exceptionally lucky that I was taught these valuable lessons at an early age and all throughout my life.

Many of the most positive influences I received reinforced this message over and over again. The incredibly famous book "How to Win Friends, and Influence People" by Dale Carnegie is pretty much a long breakdown of this simple yet incredibly important Bible verse. As a father, this verse has particular importance, because the words I choose, the things that I say in front of my children, are a huge example for them.

Even though this has been taught to me over and over again in my life, I still have my moments where I struggle with this one. Reading this verse inspires me to try harder to build my children up, as well as the people around me, no matter how big their mistakes may be. If I look in the mirror, my own mistakes are too numerous to count.

A key point to this advice is to be sincere, not just say things that you do not mean. If you cannot find positive things to say, don't make them up. Instead, focus harder on finding something, even the smallest thing to build up…trust me when I tell you, a verse like this can improve every aspect of your life as fast or faster than anything else can. Like many things that we intuitively know and understand, sometimes the difficulty is in the remembering to apply the knowledge on a daily basis. A valuable lesson that is equally effective and powerful for both business and life!

Related Movie Quote: From the Disney movie "Bambi".

Thumper: "If you can't say something nice, don't say nothing at all."("Bambi" Walt Disney Studios 1942)

The 98ᵗʰ Greatest Bible Verse – Galatians 5:13

#98 – You, my brothers, were called to be free. But do not use your freedom to indulge the sinful nature; rather serve one another in love. (Galatians 5:13)

My first note on verses like this is to point out it is just as applicable to our sisters as it is to our brothers. Many of the verses in the Bible were written at a time when things were not as equal as they are now. Often the wording is male-centric, but this does not mean it is not just as applicable to everyone, male or female. All of us were meant to be free in this life.

The challenge, as witnessed time and again with the freedoms we enjoy in America, is what people choose to do with that freedom. For example, just because one is allowed to have freedom of speech doesn't mean people should just say whatever they want. Far too often, people manipulate our freedoms to further personal agendas that have no place in the life of most good people. This verse provides great wisdom and truth. Instead of using your freedom to indulge in the sinful nature...use it to serve one another in love.

If only we could get the leaders of the world to follow advice like this, and for politicians and militaries around the world to serve one another in love. Of course, if something like that were to happen, then we would be just a little bit closer to having heaven on earth. A change like that happens one person at a time. So here's to all of us taking a moment to read a passage like this and apply it in our lives. Choosing to actually live words like this is how we can make the world a better place. For the sake of our children and our children's children, may this happen sooner rather than later.

Related Quote: "While we are free to choose our actions, we are not free to choose the consequences of our actions."

~ Stephen Covey

The 68th Greatest Bible Verse – Ephesians 6:2-3

#68 – "Honor your father and mother"– which is the first commandment with a promise –"that it may go well with you and that you may enjoy long life on the earth." (Ephesians 6:2-3)

When I was growing up, this was a verse that I tried very hard to follow. It was not always easy, but there was an innate sense of obligation to honor my parents for all that they had done for me. Having phenomenal parents made this so much easier than it is for a lot of other kids.

It is incredibly nice to know there is the huge motivational carrot of living a long life on earth as a result of it. If you can't find any other reason in your heart to honor your parents, then perhaps the thought of enjoying a long life will help you. In any case, this certainly makes for a much happier childhood, because if you treat your parents right, they will almost certainly try harder to do the best they can for you as well.

Related Quote: "A child who is allowed to be disrespectful to his parents will not have true respect for anyone."
~ Billy Graham

The 81st Greatest Bible Verse – Colossians 3:21

#81 – Fathers, do not embitter your children, or they will become discouraged. (Colossians 3:21)

Since I have entered into fatherhood status, verses like this one have become infinitely more important than they ever were before. There is a delicate balance between teaching our children discipline, strength, and work ethic and, of course, loving them and encouraging them. Too often, we get stuck pointing out our children's faults rather than celebrating their positive traits.

As it is with so many things in life, the truth is somewhere in the middle. This is a powerful lesson for all of us to take to heart. We want our children to be strong, and we need to teach them, but we need to build them up in the process, not tear them down. Finding a way to do both is vitally important, so much so that it is written in the Bible for all of us to make note of!

Related Quote: "Tell me and I forget, teach me and I may remember, involve me and I learn." ~ Benjamin Franklin

CHAPTER NINE
"THE LIST"

"The Bible is the ultimate list of how to do right, and why not to do wrong." ~ WJ Vincent II

Top Verse from "Physical"

For nothing is impossible with God. (Luke 1:37) pg. 8

Top Verse from "Spiritual"

I tell you the truth, if you have faith as small as a mustard seed, you can say to this mountain, "Move from here to there" and it will move. Nothing will be impossible for you. (Matthew 17:20-21) pg. 24

Top Verse from "Financial"

Give, and it will be given to you. A good measure, pressed down, shaken together and running over, will be poured into your lap. For with the measure you use, it will be measured to you. (Luke 6:38) pg. 44

Top Verse from "Emotional"

Even though I walk through the valley of the shadow of death, I will fear no evil, for you are with me; (Psalm 23:4) pg. 66

Top Verse from "Mental"

Listen to advice and accept instructions; and in the end you will be wise. (Proverbs 19:20) pg. 83

Top Verse from "Social"

Live in harmony with one another. Do not be proud, but be willing to associate with people of low position. Do not be conceited. (Romans 12:16) pg. 102

Top Verse from "Family"

Love is patient, love is kind. It does not envy, it does not boast, it is not proud. It is not rude, it is not self-seeking, it is not easily angered, it keeps no record of wrongs. Love does not delight in evil but rejoices with the truth. It always protects, always trusts, always hopes, always perseveres. Love never fails. (1 Corinthians 13:4-8) pg. 128

CHAPTER TEN
"ABOUT THE AUTHOR"

"The real things haven't changed. It is still best to be honest and truthful; to make the most of what we have; to be happy with simple pleasures; and have courage when things go wrong." ~ Laura Ingalls Wilder

W.J. Vincent II has spent the last 20 years of his life building businesses from start-up to success in fields as varied as Real Estate, Technology, and Environmental Health. Throughout his many different adventures, successes, and failures, certain Bible verses were always close to his heart. In January 2012, Natalia, his wife of 13 years, tragically passed away, her body having given in to her short but dramatic three-month battle with a brain tumor. Her sudden passing left W.J. a widowed father of a 1-year old baby girl and 4-year old boy of his own, along with a 12-year old boy and 15-year old girl he had been helping his mother-in-law to raise due to her battle with multiple sclerosis.

Faced with a challenge greater than any he had known, W.J. was able to find strength and inspiration from the Bible. There were many miracles and messages that saw him through the darkest moments of his life shared in this book. It is his deepest wish that The 101 Greatest Bible verses will help more people to realize, remember, or discover for the first time just how powerful and amazing the Bible is.

THANK YOU
GIFT PROMOTION

Please Visit

http://www.ThinkMoreBeMore.com

Enter Name and Email Address

or

Send an Email to:

Info@ThinkMoreBeMore.Com

and receive a special gift!

(subject to availability)

Note: A percentage of the profits of all sales of this book are donated to charity. Registering at ThinkMoreBeMore.com gives access to helping determine which charities we should support!

www.ingramcontent.com/pod-product-compliance
Lightning Source LLC
Chambersburg PA
CBHW072012040426
42447CB00009B/1599